The HOW of Leadership

The HOW of Leadership

Inspire People to Achieve Extraordinary Results

Maxwell Ubah

BUSINESS EXPERT PRESS

First published in 2018 by
Business Expert Press, LLC
222 East 46th Street, New York, NY 10017
www.businessexpertpress.com

ISBN-13: 978-1-94784-388-2 (paperback)
ISBN-13: 978-1-94784-389-9 (e-book)

Business Expert Press Human Resource Management and Organizational Behavior Collection

Collection ISSN: 1946-5637 (print)
Collection ISSN: 1946-5645 (electronic)

Cover and interior design by S4Carlisle Publishing Services Private Ltd., Chennai, India

First edition: 2018

10 9 8 7 6 5 4 3 2 1

Printed in the United States of America.

To all who desire to improve their leadership effectiveness and learn how to inspire people to achieve extraordinary results.

Abstract

No other subject determines the rise and fall of nations, organizations, families, and even individuals as leadership. No other topic determines whether people and the organizations that they work for will live up to the promise of their potential. And no other topic guarantees the future of the next generation as leadership. But how do leaders ensure that they inspire people to achieve extraordinary results for their organizations and constituencies? That's what this book intends to address.

The HOW of Leadership: Inspire People to Achieve Extraordinary Results provides a road map of how great leaders inspire people to achieve extraordinary results. It takes the confusion out of the concept of leadership and introduces easily applicable and proven leadership concepts that today's leaders can employ.

The book is divided into three sections and explores the following major themes:

Section 1—Now that You Are the Leader: This section is the foundation of leadership and focuses on six qualities that great leaders demonstrate in their character and leadership styles to first lead themselves before leading others.

Section 2—Inspire and Influence Your Team: This section focuses on the leadership strategies and tactics that leaders can use to inspire and influence their teams.

Section 3—Achieve Extraordinary Results: This section focuses on the disciplines necessary to achieve extraordinary results in organizations.

My expectation is that this book will contribute not just to the body of knowledge about leadership but to healthy and vibrant institutions making a difference in the lives of their constituents.

Keywords

extraordinary performance, inspire, leadership

Contents

Acknowledgments

There are no self-made people. We are successful because of the input and contributions of many other people in our lives. I am blessed to have a wonderful spouse and family as well as great friends, coaches, and mentors in my life. Who I am today is a reflection of the collective input of these people in my life. If I am successful today, it is because of them. And to them, I remain forever grateful.

For this particular work, I am indebted to the following people:

- Nigel Wyatt for reaching out to me about my book and the Business Expert Team for giving me the opportunity to publish with them.
- My beautiful wife, IJ, for her patience, sacrifice, understanding, and contributions as I tried to wrestle with some of the concepts and write them down. Thank you for being the sounding board for some of the ideas and for making useful suggestions.
- My mentors, life coaches, and teachers whose ideologies have shaped the person I am today. Of special note is the late Peter F. Drucker, the man who made me fall in love with management sciences even as a medical student and fueled my desire to become a management consultant.
- The executives who took time out of their busy schedules to read sections of the manuscript and make useful comments and amendments: Kennedy Uzoka, Akin Akinfemiwa, Rasheed Olaoluwa, Emeke E. Iweriebor, Valentine Ozigbo, Obi Ibekwe, Achi Innocent, Isaac Mwige, Chike Onyia, Ify Chukwuma, Samuel Nwanze, Chuks Onwuyali, Stanley Eluwa, and Abayomi Orungbe.

Introduction

Today's leaders face increasing pressures to deliver business results, perhaps more than at any other time in history. The times we are in call for a new understanding of and approach to leadership and for a new breed of leaders. With the plethora of problems being faced by today's leaders—from the pressures of globalization to cutthroat competitive challenges, from intense regulatory supervision with deregulation of industries to technological advancements and breakthroughs, including the role of artificial intelligence, from the rise of sophisticated and more discerning consumers and aggressive investors to changes in the composition of today's workforce, from social unrest to the rise of terrorist groups—they cannot afford to lead in the same way as previous generations of leaders. These challenges are a double-edged sword: They will strike deathblows to industries, markets, and companies, and in their wake, birth new industries, markets, and companies. Old paradigms, methods, and models will give way to the new. Those who remain glued to the past will wake up to find out that their successes have been confined to the ash heap of history.

Despite these challenges, the *what* of leadership—the ability to achieve results through people—remains constant; it is the *how* of leadership that's changing. Today's leaders must rise to the occasion and meet the challenges of their current realities and achieve breakthrough results by adapting to a new *how*. Critical to the new *how* of leadership is how to inspire people and teams—how to harness the creative energies of the workforce—to achieve breakthrough results.

Leadership has been defined variously by different authors and business leaders, making congruence in definition difficult. What is more important is not a new definition of leadership but a new way of looking at how leaders build enduring companies by achieving sustainable results with their constituents.

The *what* of leadership is simple—build relationships and achieve results. The *how* for each leader, however, varies. Some focus first on the discipline of achieving results and then work on developing their people to achieve the results, while others focus first on developing the relationships that will enable them to achieve the results. Both are necessary, but while the specific strategy might be different for each leader, there are however commonalities across different geographies, industries and functions. And that is what this book is about. This book has been written to address *The HOW of Leadership*—how leaders build relationships and achieve results. The book is divided into three sections, each dealing with a specific aspect of *The HOW of Leadership*.

Section 1 is the foundational section; some might call it the most important section. It is the section that focuses on you, the leader. There is a paradox of leadership: Leadership begins with you, your hopes, and aspirations but leadership is not about you. In this section, we will explore six topics to get the foundation of leadership right.

Section 2 looks at how the leader inspires his people. Having laid the foundation in the previous section, this section will discuss five things that the leader is supposed to do (in addition to everything covered in Section 1) to inspire people to achieve results. There are many things a leader can do to inspire his people but these five are critical. Ignore them at your peril.

Section 3 focuses on performance. Ultimately, leadership is about achieving results. This section will cover nine essentials a leader must focus on to achieve extraordinary results.

As it were, we have focused on the Person of the leader (Section 1), the People he is leading (Section 2), the Process of leading (Sections 2 and 3), and end result of leadership—the Performance expected (Section 3)—or what I call the 4Ps of leadership. It is a simple yet revolutionary concept. We can say that a leader leads his people through a process to achieve performance expectations. Therefore, the starting point of leadership is the person of the leader; the end goal is performance expectations. In between are the people involved and the process of leadership. And every time a leader fails (performance), if you look closely, you will find that at least one of the 4Ps is missing—either in the person of the leader or in the people in the team or in the process of influencing and motivating people or building a team or in the achievement of business outcomes or desired results. Either way, one or more of the puzzle pieces of the 4Ps are missing in situations of leadership failure.

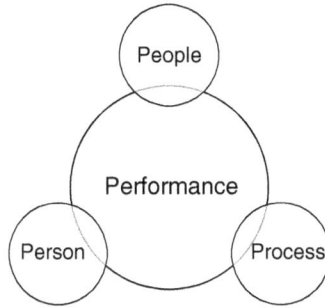

Although leadership is not positional, this book will help both positional and nonpositional leaders to improve their leadership effectiveness within the context of their organizational results, irrespective of the nature of their organizations—private, public, or nonprofit. Irrespective of the pronoun used -(he, his, him or she, her), leadership is not gender specific. Leadership or leading effectively is for everyone.

I'd love to hear from you. I hope this book will serve as the catalyst to give your own leadership potential the needed push and help you to improve on your leadership effectiveness—in your own unique way.

SECTION 1

Now that You Are the Leader

Leadership happens only when there are *purposeful* and *positive interactions* between the leader and the led that inspire the latter to achieve extraordinary results or *high performance*. Great leaders know that every interaction with their followers is an opportunity to inspire them to achieve extraordinary results whether the interaction is face-to-face, through e-mail, or by phone. The goal is the same: to inspire their followers to achieve breakthrough results. Purposeful and positive interactions between the leader and the led are the means of leadership; high performance is its end or goal.

This concept of leadership, in my view, is encapsulated in the following equation:

$$\text{Leadership} = \text{relationships} \times \text{results}$$

Every definition of leadership can be summarized by this equation. It is my working definition of leadership. So simple yet so powerful. Leaders build people (teams) and achieve results. Nothing can be simpler than that!

Using the relationships-and-results dimensions of leadership, we can easily identify three false leadership states—boss, friend, and stranger—as captured in the matrix that follows:

	Results	
High Relationships	Friend "Nice Guy"	Leader
Low Relationships	Stranger	Boss "Macho Image"
	Low	High

A *boss* focuses more on performance at the expense of the relational dimension of leadership. He is more concerned with the work output than the welfare of his people. He can be counted upon to deliver business results but will leave people burned out in the process. Most companies run the boss-like model of leadership—working conditions are horrible, performance targets are unrealistic, and threats of sack are used to motivate people to keep delivering on those unrealistic targets.

A *friend* focuses more on the relational dimension at the expense of results. A friend is more concerned about your welfare than your work output. You enjoy the company of a friend but won't trust him with critical and sensitive organizational issues. The challenge with a friend is that the means (people) become the end. As long as the people are happy even though performance is suffering, a friendly leader is satisfied. This type of leader will not make the tough calls for the organization to succeed if they will somehow affect those relationships.

A *stranger* is the worst of both worlds—at least you know what you are getting from a friend or boss. A stranger does not build relationships or accomplish results. He is cold, aloof, emotionally volatile, incompetent, and lacks the follow through to achieve business results.

A *leader*, on the other hand, achieves results and drives performance through people. He harnesses the power of relationships to deliver outstanding results. He combines the attitude of a boss, relentlessly focusing on performance, with that of a friend, creating healthy, collaborative relationships with his team. Consequently, a leader is more than a friend and more than a boss. He is also more than an individual contributor—one who achieves results by the force of his personality and the strength of his skills. He achieves results only through people, people who become better and more productive and more satisfied under his watch, people who will eventually call him their *leader!*

This section covers six topics:

- Leadership: It's not about you!
- You are your first follower!
- Decisiveness
- Love what you do, whom you do it with, and whom you do it for
- Service-oriented leadership
- How will you be remembered?

CHAPTER 1

Leadership: It's Not about You!

Leadership begins with attitude. No title or position can make a true leader out of a man with a negative attitude.

It's Not about You!

Michael is aggressive and very competitive by nature. He likes the spotlight and is not afraid of confronting problems or people headlong. Due to his aggressive nature, he can be counted upon to achieve business results. The challenge, however, is that Michael doesn't care about people's feelings in the process. He is impatient with people he considers slow learners or who do not see things from his perspective, and usually, it is either his way or the highway. He is a classic workplace bully. He has been promoted to the position of a branch manager. Will Michael make a good leader?

While ambition can guarantee personal success, ambition alone cannot guarantee effective leadership. Without ambition—the personal drive or desire for success—individuals cannot succeed, but without the right attitude, they cannot become effective leaders. We have established that leadership is relationships $\times$ results. Leaders who fail to maintain the right balance between ambition for results and the right attitude of developing positive relationships with their constituents will eventually lose their leadership effectiveness. So, while Michael may possibly achieve results in the short to medium term, he will not achieve sustainable results in the long term unless he changes his attitude. The lesson is obvious: Unrestrained ambition or oversized ego destroys!

All leaders are ambitious, but the focus of their ambitions is what differentiates great leaders from ordinary leaders. Great leaders are incredibly ambitious, but so are mediocre leaders. The difference is that great leaders are ambitious about their organizations. They have subsumed their personal ambitions for the greater good of their organizations and nations. Their ambitions—build a world-class company, lead the market, and achieve breakthrough results—can be witnessed through their organization's success. To these leaders, leadership is about building enduring institutions that will consistently outperform their competitors. They take a long-term view of leadership and leading.

Both Andrew Grove of Intel and Steve Jobs of Apple Inc. commented that their greatest achievements were in building a strong company. Grove, in an interview with *Nightly Business Report* coanchor Susie Gharib said, "My proudest accomplishment has been to contribute to the creation of a company that has helped put a billion PCs into people's hands."[1] Was he ambitious? Of course! But his ambition was channeled into building a great company—attitude. For ordinary leaders, however, their ambitions are for their own personal gain—their personal benefits at the expense of their institutions and the people they are meant to serve. To these second group of leaders, life and leadership are all about them, just like it is with Michael.

In his best-selling book *Good to Great: Why Some Companies Make the Leap and Others Don't*, Jim Collins wrote about this same concept. Writing about what he termed "Level 5" leadership, the first ingredient necessary to transform a good company into a great company, he noted,

> Level 5 leaders channel their ego needs away from themselves and into the larger goal of building a great company. It's not that Level 5 leaders have no ego or self-interest. Indeed, they are incredibly ambitious—but their ambition is first and foremost for the institution, not themselves.

It's Time to Grow Up

I have seen this negative, overambitious attitude play out at the personal, organizational, and national levels. And every time I see it, I can always predict that such individuals and the organizations that they run or the nations they preside over are doomed to mediocrity and failure as there is usually no hope for people who think that life and leadership are all about them. When we think that we are the center of the universe, we show how small our world is and how immature and childish our understanding of leadership and life is because a child simply thinks only about herself.

A country is doomed if its leader is immature and its high officials throw parties in the morning.

—Ancient Wisdom

In a child's world, only one person exists—her. Every other person is secondary. It's all about her, her desires, and her wants, just like Michael. But as the child begins to grow, a transition happens: She begins to see life from others' perspectives. She learns that the family is not just about her, that others do not exist just to make her happy. The growth in perspective happens when the child now learns that life ultimately is not just about her.

Just as a child's growth always comes with a change in perspectives, leadership development and maturity happen when our perspectives on leadership change—when we understand that it is not just all about us. In life and in leadership, we all start out as children, emotionally immature and selfish, thinking only about our own wants, desires, and goals. We listen to only one station, WII-FM, an acronym that stands for "What's in it for me?" But as we grow, we come to see the needs, dreams, and aspirations of other members of the team.

There are two characteristics of leadership growth and maturity. The first is *consideration*. We begin to think about others—their feelings, fears, and views. Today, this concept is called diversity. The second is *inclusion*. When we consider others, we include them in our plans, and include their views before arriving at a decision. The result of consideration and inclusion is the ability to subordinate one's desires for the greater good of the team. Consideration and inclusion help us pursue a course that will be beneficial to everybody in the team and not only ourselves. You know that someone is growing and will likely make a good leader when his language changes from "I" to "We," from "What I want" to "What we—the team—wants." So sorry, Michael, you won't make a good leader!

The leaders who work most effectively, it seems to me, never say "I." And that's not because they have trained themselves not to say "I." They don't think "I." They think "we"; they think "team." They understand their job to be is to make the team function. They accept responsibility and don't sidestep it, but "we" gets the credit. This is what creates trust, what enables you to get the task done.

—Peter F. Drucker

Individuals with skills but without the right attitude will not realize their potentials, and individuals with ambition but without the self-restraint of a positive attitude will self-destruct. Michael's career will be derailed if he doesn't learn this lesson and make the necessary adjustments on time.

Lasting success is impossible without the right attitude. While attitude alone doesn't guarantee success, true and lasting success is impossible without it. I see attitude as the trim tab that determines whether potential will be harnessed and realized. Most leaders fail not because they do not have the potential for success but simply because their attitude of and understanding about leadership undermined their ability to succeed.

$$success = potential \times attitude$$

What exactly is attitude? It is a mindset, a way of thinking that manifests in behaviors. It is your understanding (or lack thereof) about an issue that shapes your views and governs your pursuits. It is your disposition about life, people, and circumstances in general. It is your biases, assumptions, and prejudices that color your understanding of and response to situations. In aeronautics, it is "the position of the aircraft orspacecraft relative to a frame of reference (the horizon or direction of motion)".[2] That is, the attitude of the airplane reflects the direction of movement of the plane. Consequently, the direction of your life followsyour personal attitude. If I know your attitude about an issue, I can almost always predict your behaviors in that context.

Wrong Attitudes toward Leadership

Since this is a book about leadership and not about attitude in general, the focus will be on the wrong attitudes toward leadership. I see two major wrong attitudes toward leadership.

Leadership Is about Positions and Titles

A great misunderstanding about leadership today is the impression that leadership is all about positions and titles. We call people who have titles "leaders." Nothing can be further from the truth. Although titles confer some measure of positional authority on individuals, they don't confer leadership. This is due to the fact that positional authority is usually formal, it resides in the position and not in the person, consequently, followership is forced not voluntary. True leaders may sometimes have positions and titles, but it wasn't their positions and titles that made them leaders. They are leaders because of who they are and what they did for others.

Look at it this way—a male is different from a man. Being a male is determined by your sex chromosomes; being a man is determined by your sense of responsibility and maturity. So are positions and leadership. Leadership is beyond having titles; it is developing the sense of responsibility and discharging your duties with or without titles. Leaders in all spheres of life are individuals who choose to accept responsibility for others for their benefit.

> True leadership is not about occupying a position but fulfilling a purpose, a purpose that uplifts the human spirit in that generation, organization, or community.

Leadership is about responsibility, not titles. Your position doesn't make you a leader; your sense of responsibility does. *Leadership is always measured by impact, not titles.* Leaders add value to others; they don't accumulate titles for themselves. When we think of leaders like Nelson Mandela, Mother Teresa, and Bill Gates do we remember them because of the titles or positions they occupied or because of the impact they made? Leadership is about making a difference. If your life makes a portion of your world a bit better and uplifts the human spirit by inspiring it to reach for the stars, then you are a leader irrespective of your current position and title.

To make the world a bit better, to contribute your quota, and to leave your footprints as a guide for the next generation are at the heart of leadership. And if you don't, then you are not a leader irrespective of your title. When we think that leadership is positional, we will do everything in our power to get our dream position, and once we get it, we will do everything in our power to protect the position. Leadership then becomes a destination, not a journey. The do-or-die mentality in despotic politics is a manifestation of this erroneous belief that leadership and position are synonymous. Turf wars, silo mentality, and organizational fiefdom are also telltale signs of an organization filled with people who think that leadership is about positions and titles.

Leadership Is About Having Power over People

Just as leadership is not about positions and titles, it is also not about power over people. Leadership is about influence, and influence transcends power to personhood—who you are. To truly measure your influence, ask yourself what people will do for you without your position or power. Many centuries ago, a wise king discovered that a leader who lacks understanding is very oppressive.[3] This kind of leader has position and power, but because he does not understand the essence of true leadership, he uses the power to oppress the people he is meant to serve, appoints his cronies, and changes the laws of the land in order to perpetuate himself in office.

The dictatorial tendencies, oppression, and corporate bullying in many organizations are symptomatic of the lack of understanding of what real leadership is. In such organizations, people live in fear and spend more time managing these so-called leaders than doing their jobs. Real leaders understand that power is to be used only for one purpose—to advance the goals of their organizations or nations for the benefit of their people. And the greatest form of power is the power that resides in your person (your knowledge, skill, character, and strength of relationships) and not in your position. That is, who you are is more powerful than where you sit in the organization. The latter is transient, while the former is permanent.

> Real leaders understand that power is to be used only for one purpose—to advance the goals of their organisations or nations for the benefit of their people.

A wrong attitude hordes power as if it were a scarce commodity, leading to fear, intimidation, lack of initiative and a sense of helplessness on the part of the followers. It cripples the drive to succeed and plunges organizations toward bankruptcy. Think of North Korea and other purely communist countries. Some modern organizations are no different. Power is so concentrated at the top that people become immobilized and must wait for orders from superiors to lift a pin. The right attitude toward leadership shares power at appropriate levels, leading to empowered and motivated staff who go out and achieve breakthrough results.

Manifestations of the Wrong Attitudes toward Leadership

The two common behavioral manifestations of the wrong attitudes toward leadership are as follows:

Superstar Syndrome

Superstars feed on the steroid of attention. They want to be the center of the universe in their teams or organizations. They think they are superior to everyone else. Without them, the team or organization will not succeed. Because they think they are the most important people in their teams, they want to be treated with utmost respect, assigned the best accounts, granted all their wishes, and given the first choice in everything. Their needs take precedence over the organization's needs.

The most common manifestations of the superstar syndrome are *selfishness*, *arrogance*, and *pride* (SAP). Some other manifestations are as follows:

- They have the final say in every conversation as they are always right.
- They must win every argument or force the superiority of their ideas on others.
- They are dismissive and disrespectful of others openly because they think others are inferior to them. Remember Hitler's Aryan blood?
- They shoot down other people's ideas, especially when these ideas are contrary to theirs. They are vicious in attacking others who dare to hold a contrary opinion from theirs. Disagree with them and you are branded "Enemy of the State."

- They form cliques with themselves at the center.
- They develop a paranoid mindset that the enemy is within—everybody else inside the organization is either a potential competitor to take away a portion of their pie or a potential thief and should not be trusted. They live by the rule that putting out others' candles enhances the brightness of theirs. Internal strife, low trust, feelings of suspicion, and excessive controls are common manifestations of the "enemy is within" mindset.

Messianic Complex

The messianic complex is the superstar syndrome taken to the extreme. Usually it happens when the superstar syndrome has been left unchecked. Such people now think that they are the "saviors" of their worlds; without them, the team, organization, or nation will disintegrate. And because they think they are the promised messiahs, they want to be worshipped. They expect and demand absolute loyalty because they are sovereign and develop an infallibility complex because they think they are above the law and above making mistakes, all symptoms of autocratic dictatorship. They do not tolerate dissenting views and will use everything at their disposal to put out the fires of opposition. They are impatient with people because messiahs don't suffer fools gladly. Mobutu Sese Seko, Idi Amin and Robert Mugabe readily comes to mind.

Other manifestations include but are not limited to the following:

- They do all the talking, and people respond only when asked because sovereigns speak and subjects listen and applaud.
- They take all the credit as nobody else is good enough without them, and they shift all the blame as they are too perfect to either make a mistake or fail. They never say sorry or apologize. Messiahs are infallible.
- They operate a caste system: Royalty does not mingle with ordinary folks. Nepotism is their stock in trade.

The first test of great leadership begins with attitude, not ambition or potential. And the attitude is first and foremost for the organization or nation, and not for oneself. The willingness to make personal sacrifices for the good of the organization is the starting point of great leadership. Paradoxically, the more you put your organization or others first, the more you achieve greatness and are celebrated by society and called a leader.

Be careful of any individual who is highly ambitious about getting to the throne or a position. People who fight for positions have nothing else to offer. Great leaders are usually not ambitious for positions or power but are forced by situations and circumstances and the plight of the human condition to accept the responsibility of leading their people.

A great leader represents his constituents (people, organization, nation and their interests) effectively.

Archbishop Desmond Tutu noted that he is a leader by choice because nature abhors a vacuum. Great leaders accept the position because they have to—the vacuum has to be filled—and not primarily because they want to, but they accept the responsibility of leadership because they want to. Ordinary and mediocre leaders, on the other hand, take the position because they want to but fail to take up the responsibility that the position entails and are consequently voted out or removed by the board or shareholders.

A Leader, a Representative

I see a close similarity between great leaders and great lawyers. A lawyer's greatness has nothing to do with her educational qualifications or how long she has been in practice. A lawyer's greatness is simply measured by her win–loss ratio. Her greatness is tied to her representing her clients effectively—helping them to win. When she stands in the law court, it is with only one goal—to point the judge/jury to her client and get the best possible deal for him or her. As her client wins, she wins. In a similar manner, a leader's greatness is tied to her ability to effectively represent her team, organization, or constituents. As the team, organization, or constituency wins, she wins. As she channels her energy to helping the team win, she is celebrated by the team as their leader. But if she tries to force the team to help her achieve her own personal greatness, she repels them and falters and fails in her leadership quest.

Leadership is leaders acting—as well as caring, inspiring and persuading others to act—for certain shared goals that represent the values—the wants and needs, the aspirations and expectations—of themselves and the people they represent.

—James MacGregor Burns, *Leadership*

The leadership spirit begins with attitude, not ambition. The question we should ask is not whether you are ambitious but "What's your ambition for or about?"

My Commitment

"I commit to developing the right attitude toward leadership."

Now go ahead and write specific ways to achieve the commitment you've made.

1. _____
2. _____
3. _____

CHAPTER 2

You Are Your First Follower

History's great achievers—a Napoleon, a da Vinci, a Mozart—have always managed themselves. That, in large measure, is what made them great achievers.

—Peter F. Drucker, *The Effective Executive*

Sometimes leaders are so hung up on getting followers and motivating people that they forget that they are their first followers. You are the best advertisement for your dream. People look first at the person of the leader before they look to his dreams and strategic intent or vision statements. When people lack faith in the leader, they won't believe in his dreams and join the cause. When we announce our bold vision and try to attract people to our dreams, they ask the following questions: Are you the kind of leader I can trust? Are you the kind I would want to follow? Can I see it in your life? Do you exemplify the commitment you want from me?

So, leadership is about being the brand ambassador of your dream, the mirror through which people understand what you expect from them. Without you being a follower of your dreams and the principles you espouse, people might follow you temporarily, but sooner than later they will find out that you are a hypocrite and leave in droves. Remember the famous quote that "you can fool all the people some of the time and some of the people all the time, but you cannot fool all the people all the time?"

To become a great leader, you need to remember the following foundational leadership principles:

- *Your ability to lead people cannot be greater than your capacity to follow.* Every leader is first a follower of principles. We are both leaders and followers at the same time. Every leader has followers and has someone or a group or even the constitution above him to follow. The president of a country, the highest position in any country, leads the whole nation but must be a follower of the constitution. If he cannot abide by the constitution, he cannot lead. So, if the president, the highest official in a country, is both a leader and a follower at the same time, no individual exists only in a leadership capacity. We both lead and follow at the same time.

- *To expect people to follow us beyond our capacity to lead is witchcraft.* Some leaders, without developing their capacity to lead, want people to follow them blindly just because they have a position or even vision. With a gun to people's head, they will follow you beyond your capacity to lead. They are not really following you; they are coerced by the gun to follow. And as soon as they find the slightest opportunity to escape, they will. People will not be attracted to you if you have not developed your capacity to lead. And at the slightest opportunity, they will leave you.

- *The first responsibility of a leader is to himself.* We must become the best advertisement of our dreams, the kind of leader that others will willingly follow. Why? *Because we influence people from the strength of our character and the depth of our convictions.* Without focusing on yourself, you cannot become a great leader. Manage yourself well, and you are ready to lead others. Most times, when leaders fail, they fail because of character issues—emotional volatility, greed, unbridled libido, and so on (factors that self-management would have dealt with long before the leaders started to lead others). When others see how well you have managed yourself, they give you the permission to lead them.

Understanding the Leadership Journey

It is a cliché that leadership is a journey but what people fail to appreciate is that the leadership journey is first and foremost inward (with yourself, your person, beliefs, and character) before it is outward (with others). When I teach leadership to organizations, I ask the participants what is the first question people ask when someone invites them to embark with him or her on a journey. The answer I always get is, "Where are we going?" That is a question of destination. However, I tell them that that is the second question people ask. The first has been answered internally before this second question. Usually, I see the surprise on their faces. I inform them that the first question people ask themselves when someone invites them on a journey is, "Who Are You?" Until I am satisfied with the *who* question, the *where* or even the *why* question doesn't arise. What do I mean? You wouldn't ask a stranger the *where* question, would you? No. The question you will ask is *who are you?* Until we are satisfied with the who question, we do not ask the where and why question.

Often leaders fail to get this. They are communicating grandiose visions and strategic directions and painting colorful dreams about the future; they even hire executive coaches to teach them how to deliver powerful speeches, develop stage presence and charisma, but they forget that the most powerful speech delivered through an untrustworthy vessel will not be received or received at best with skepticism. They have not answered the who question before trying to explain the where question.

The first part of the leadership journey is the journey of managing one's self. It is about the who question. It is taking a look at what Michael Jackson called the "Man in the Mirror" and asking yourself the hard question, Why should they follow me?

The second part of the leadership journey is taking others along on that journey and making the journey enjoyable for them. Most books on leadership are focused on the second part of the leadership journey, ignoring the first part, but this book and a handful of others are different. Dag Hammarskjöld, former secretary-general of the United Nations, rightly noted, "We have become adept at exploring outer space, but we have not developed similar skills in exploring our own personal inner spaces. In fact, the longest journey is the journey inward."

Early leadership experts focused on the first part of the leadership journey. Leadership is self-development before people development. But somewhere along the line, we missed it with disastrous consequences.

Little wonder with all the books on leadership out there, leadership is still the most pressing need of the world today.

> Most powerful is he who has himself in his power. (Lucius Annaeus Seneca)

> He that would govern others first should be master of himself. (Philip Massinger)

> He who has control over his spirit is greater than he who takes over the city. (Solomon)

To help you in journeying inward and managing yourself, I have what I termed the IDEAL framework to get you started. You can add to it.

I—Integrity

The place of integrity in leadership cannot be overemphasized. Arthur Andersen LLP, Enron, and Parmalat all fell from their lofty heights because of the absence of integrity. On a personal note, Judas Iscariot, Harvey Weinstein, and Dr. Larry Nassar all fell, too, because of a lack of integrity. Without integrity, any success achieved is temporary and fleeting at best. Integrity is the bedrock upon which sustainable success is built. It is the foundation of true and lasting greatness.

What is integrity? Integrity is from the root word *integer*, which means whole or complete. It means to have undivided attention or having the highest ethical and moral standards. It also means to be integrated, having all aspects of one's life under control. Dr. Larry Nassar, the disgraced U.S. doctor who had abused over 168 gymnasts, was an intelligent doctor but his life was not complete or integrated. His unbridled passion and lust led to his downfall. Same with Harvey Weinstein. An aspect of their life ran unchecked and ended up destroying the other parts.

Why is integrity important in leadership? Because of its relationship to trust. Trust is the glue that binds followers and leaders together. Trust is to human relationships what honey is to bees. But without integrity, trust cannot be built. Integrity is the foundation of trust. What is the relationship between the two? Integrity is personal or behavioral; it is keeping consistently one's word, promises and abiding by a set of moral or ethical values. Trust, on the other hand, is relational.

It is seen in expectations. Can I take you at your word? Will you cover for me? Would you defend my interest? Trust is a perception formed by integrity. Thus, without integrity, trust is impossible. Without trust, enduring relationships are impossible. And without enduring relationships, leadership is a mirage. A whole chapter is dedicated to the issue of trust in organizations (Chapter 13).

To get started, integrity has three major components:

- *Your behaviors—embody personal and organizational values:* Examples are more potent than lectures. Do you know what is the greatest motivational principle in the universe? *The power of a positive example.* What we see others do is far more powerful than what we hear them say. Great leaders lead by examples. They hold themselves to a higher standard than what others expect of them. They exemplify the principles they require from their people. They know that people will not do what they say or even preach but will do what they see them do. They walk the talk.

  Integrity is seen in your behaviors. Your behaviors are governed by your values and beliefs. Great leaders have high moral values. Leaders who lack personal values or fail to embody their organizational values will lose the moral right to lead others. Scott Berkun aptly captured it when he wrote,

  > I think that leadership comes from integrity—that you do whatever you ask others to do. I think there are non-obvious ways to lead. Just by providing a good example as a parent, a friend, a neighbor makes it possible for other people to see better ways to do things. Leadership does not need to be a dramatic, fist in the air and trumpets blaring, activity.[4]

  Leadership is not neutral. It is values laden and values driven. Without embodying personal and organizational values, you will not get off the starting block in your leadership journey. Call it credibility, truthfulness, honesty, or trustworthiness; no one will follow a leader who does not exemplify the organizational values. However, when organizational values conflict with their values, great leaders take the high road of personal excellence rather than compromise on their values.

- *Your work—deliver personal excellence:* You were promoted to a leadership position to achieve results through others. You are not some football coach shouting instructions from the touchline, instead you are a player–manager: You have your own responsibilities too while trying to achieve results through others. You must enter the ring and contribute your quota, and your team members must see that you have a positive attitude toward work and discipline. Leaders who do not contribute to the work but prefer to just shout instructions will not last as leaders. Leaders who drop the ball in their own assignments cannot encourage and motivate others to achieve results. Being an example also includes delivering on your tasks with excellence. And excellence is delivered through your skills and your work habits, not through your speeches. Your skills indicate what you can do; your work habits show how you work and how hard you work. Eloquence is no substitute for hard work and discipline. All the talk about smart work is good, but I am yet to see any person who achieved anything worthy of note without some measure of hard work. A skillful leader with poor work habits—procrastination, tardiness, untidiness—will be hampered not by his skills but by his work habits. Both must be managed. So, you need to constantly hone your skills and watch how you work as a leader. One of the greatest indictments I have heard as a facilitator concerning a leader was after I finished a training on *achieving personal excellence.* A participant walked up to me and sought my advice. He asked me,

  > How do I manage my boss? He is so slow and work grinds to a halt when he is around. But as soon as he is away on a vacation, for example, we (the team) get more done in his absence.

  My heart sank. If people can achieve more in the absence of the boss because his presence is a clog in the wheel, then he needs to be fired! Peter Drucker puts it this way: "Effective leadership is not about making speeches or being liked; leadership is defined by results, not attributes."

- *Keeping confidences:* Your position as a leader will grant you privileged access to information both organizational and your staff's private hopes, struggles, and fears. Integrity means you should treasure that information and not use it to your own advantage (organizational) or use it against your people. Once you begin to abuse your privileged access, you lose the right to be called a leader. As in the case of a doctor or a priest, such information should be held in confidence. Keeping confidences is knowing that not all organizational information should be shared with others even in the same organization.

D—Decisiveness

The next chapter is devoted to the need for leaders to be decisive. Leadership requires the leader to make certain decisions for the good of the team and the organization—decisions that might be unpopular in the short term. The ability to withstand pressure and to not cave in to popular demands is a hallmark of great leaders. Winston Churchill would have surrendered England's sovereignty had it not been for this quality. Nelson Mandela would have accepted temporary freedom instead of seeing a South Africa free from apartheid had it not been for this quality. To decide to do what is right and to stand by it is far more important than to be liked as a leader!

E—Emotional Energy

Leaders are usually promoted to positions of authority because of their technical competence. Such technical competence, while still relevant, is not sufficient for them to lead effectively as they need to develop the ability to work with and through people. A leader is more than an individual contributor; he achieves results through people. And central to the ability to work with and through people is the leader's ability to manage his emotions. Nowhere is managing one's emotions more critical than in a leadership role—with people.

Let's face it. Leadership is a difficult and messy challenge because it deals with people above, across, and below within the organization. People, we know, are irrational, unpredictable, and difficult to deal with. They will task your emotional energy and leave you frustrated and exasperated. Also, leaders today are under a lot of pressure—from customers, shareholders, and competitors. And such high-pressure situations usually task one's emotional energy. If you do not know how to manage your emotions, you will become emotionally volatile, throwing tantrums around for every little mistake, and will be perceived as a weak leader.

Think for a moment: Will you want to be led by someone who has no control over his emotions, who screams at the slightest mistake and pours out obscenities at his followers? I bet you that the answer is a resounding "No." You cannot be an effective leader without managing your emotions, for a leader's *emotional energy* sets the tone for the interactions between him and his team and determines the mood or atmosphere of his team, which eventually affects the motivational readiness score of the team.

Managing one's emotions is the domain of *emotional intelligence*, a phrase coined by Peter Salovey and John Mayer but made popular by Daniel Goleman, author of the *New York Times* and *Wall Street Journal* best seller *Emotional Intelligence.* In its simplest terms, emotional intelligence is about understanding and managing one's emotions and those of others to achieve the desired results.

Here's my chart (Figure 2.1), from observing myself and other leaders around the world, to show the link between a leader's emotions and the organizational climate and results.

Consequently, improving organizational results requires that leaders manage their emotional energy and keep an eye on their moods and behaviors (interactions and conversations) with their teams.

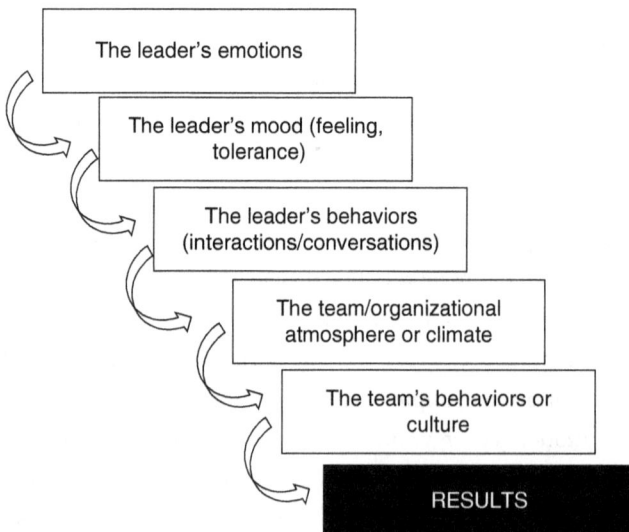

Figure 2.1 How a leader's emotions affects organizational results

A—Attitude

This book began with the importance of attitude and rates attitude over ambition. Nobody will follow you as a leader if they think you will use them to achieve your personal aims. Your attitude answers the question, "Why do you want to lead the people?" I have discovered that many people want positions because of the power, prominence, prestige, and pride that such positions confer and not because they love people. The primary motive for accepting leadership responsibility is to ensure the benefit of the people you are meant to lead. While your organization will provide your position, only people can make you a leader.

I see leadership as the privilege conferred on individuals by their followers, whom they have influenced and inspired. As in the case of a non-hereditary chieftaincy title or an honorary degree, only the people you have influenced positively can confer the title of a leader on you. Where you sit in the organizational chart doesn't make you a leader. What the people say about you is what makes you a leader.

L—Leadership Style

Leadership is situational. The context determines the appropriate leadership style and behaviors. While Winston Churchill was celebrated as a wartime hero, he lost the elections after the war. The appropriate leadership style required after the war was building coalitions and partnerships across parties in order to rebuild Great Britain and not the coercive or autocratic style required for war. Leaders who fail to read their environmental or business context and adjust their styles appropriately will lose their leadership effectiveness.

Effective leaders use different leadership styles for different situations and different leadership styles for different individuals in the same situation, depending on the individuals involved. A one-size-fits-all approach will not work. Think of it this way: The acceleration capacity of a car is fixed by the manufacturer, but the speed is determined by the driver on the basis of several factors—the nature of the road, the traffic on the road, familiarity with the road, and the sense of urgency of the driver. So, while capacity is fixed, the driver determines how fast or slow to go. In a similar vein, while your personality is fixed, your leadership style should be determined by the situation and the people involved. Without adjusting your leadership style to the situation and the people involved, you will erode your leadership effectiveness.

Daniel Goleman in a *Harvard Business Review* article (March 2000) titled "Leadership That Gets Results" postulates that effective leaders use six different leadership styles to achieve results: *coercive, authoritative, affiliative, democratic, pacesetting, and coaching*. These styles, according to Goleman, are used in the following contexts:

- Coercive—used to demand compliance
- Authoritative—used to mobilize people toward a vision
- Affiliative—used to build harmony and trust
- Democratic—used to build consensus
- Pacesetting—used to set high standards of performance
- Coaching—used to develop staff

Effective leaders choose from the basket of leadership styles to address their people and situation and achieve the desired results. That's one difference between effective leaders and mediocre leaders: They know the appropriate style to deploy depending on the person or the situation. They have situational awareness, a sixth sense that tells them which style is appropriate.

My Commitment

"I commit to becoming the kind of leader that others will want to follow."

Now go ahead and write specific ways to achieve the commitment you've made.

1. _____
2. _____
3. _____

CHAPTER 3

Decisiveness

If I had to sum up in one word the qualities that make a good manager,
I'd say that it all comes down to decisiveness.

—Lee Iacocca, *Iacocca: An Autobiography*

What Would You Do?

You are the branch manager of Bank X and Ade is your number one staff. In fact, he is the major reason why your branch is profitable as he has the branch's most profitable accounts, accounts he brought to the bank from his previous bank when he joined your bank.

Recently, you have been hearing information about him sexually harassing some junior staff. You have discussed the situation with him and he denied the allegations. Having no concrete evidence, you asked him to desist from such if the allegations were true.

This fateful day, unbeknownst to him, you caught him trying to harass one of the cleaners and she screamed that Ade shouldn't touch her. That's when you cleared your throat. And he saw you.

You are his boss. The sanction grid requires that he resigns or his appointed is terminated. If you recommend it, you will lose the customers (and accounts) he brought and likely become a loss-making branch. What would you do?

The litmus test for great leadership is the ability to make decisions and stand by them. Ordinary people rarely make effective decisions, and even when they do, they vacillate under pressure. Who would you like to have as a leader—one who cannot make decisions and keeps postponing crucial issues for fear of making a mistake or one who stands up in difficult situations and makes the tough calls that are necessary? I am sure that you will choose the latter over the former, no matter how nice and gentle he may be.

We may appreciate leaders for their humility, but it is their toughness during times of crisis that galvanizes us to them. A leader must balance a tender heart with a tough skin—the heart of a dove with the skin of a rhinoceros. The tender heart is for people, and the tough skin is for problems.

History (whether personal, organizational, or national) is shaped by decisions—from the decision to sign the Declaration of Independence to the decision to send a man to the moon to the decision to not give up the seat in a bus. Show me any great leader, and I will show you one who can make the tough calls and stand by them. Study the lives of great men and women, and you will find that at seminal moments in their lives, they made the tough decisions and stood by them. The world might at first have ridiculed them but later realized that they are individuals with grit and then embraced them as true leaders.

> We may appreciate leaders for their humility, but it is their toughness during times of crisis that galvanizes us to them.

Andrew Grove, in his book *Only the Paranoid Survive: How to Exploit the Crisis Points That Challenge Every Company*, mentions two critical moments in the life of Intel—what he called *strategic inflection points*—that defined its corporate destiny. The first was moving Intel away from the memory chip business because of the pressure of Japanese chipmakers. Intel was the dominant maker of memory chips in the 1970s. However, in the early 1980s, Japanese chipmakers eroded Intel's dominance principally because of relatively low-priced but high-quality chips.

As hard as Intel tried, it could not catch up with the Japanese chipmakers. It was at a crossroads. The company had lost its bearings and momentum. Its cash cow was now on death row, no thanks to the Japanese. A decision had to be made. The middle of 1985 was a watershed moment for the company. Grove wrote in the book,

> I was in my office with Intel's chairman and CEO, Gordon Moore, and we were discussing our quandary. Our mood was downbeat. I looked out the window . . . then I turned back to Gordon and I asked, "If we got kicked out and the board brought in a new

CEO, what do you think he would do?" Gordon answered without hesitation, "He would get us out of memories." I stared at him, numb, then said, "Why shouldn't you and I walk out the door, come back and do it ourselves?"[5]

That decision became the turning point of Intel as a company. Although the transformation did not come without its own pains, the company was able to make the transition, and today Intel is recognized as the leading brand in microprocessors. The second decision was to take a write-down of $475 million because of a rounding error in one of their Pentium microprocessor chips that "an average spreadsheet user will encounter only once in 27,000 years of spreadsheet use."[6]

These two decisions secured Intel's future and dominance of the microprocessor market going into the 21st century. Had Grove not made the tough calls, perhaps Intel's story would have been different.

A leader who is not comfortable with making the tough calls or one who easily vacillates in his opinions and decisions will erode his leadership effectiveness. Who will want to follow such a leader in times of crisis? During times of economic boom, people will easily forgive such a leader. But in times of crisis, the times we are in, his leadership will be questioned, his people will become confused, and customers will leave in droves. When BlackBerry co-CEOs tottered during the rapid growth of the iPhone and the emergence of Android leaders like Samsung, customers left in droves.

It is my personal belief that the strength of leadership lies in the ability to make tough decisions. When I talk about the ability to make tough decisions, I need to quickly clarify that it is more than just speed in decision making, although speed can sometimes be very crucial. However, speed alone is not enough; the quality of the decision is far more important. Nobody feels comfortable following an impetuous leader who quickly jumps to conclusions and makes critical decisions without gathering all the facts that are necessary for such decisions. Such a leader will lead his organization and people hurtling down a cliff in destruction. Being decisive means not only having the ability to make quick decisions but also having a clear framework that enables you and your followers to make the right decisions. Providing clarity of purpose and direction that enables your team to make the right decisions is an important quality of being a decisive leader.

Why Do Some Leaders Fail to Be Decisive?

They Do Not Understand the Responsibility of Leadership

I mentioned earlier that the strength of leadership lies in the ability to make tough decisions. The dividing line between great and weak leaders lies in this attribute. Without learning the discipline of decision making, your leadership will be handicapped. In fact, your leadership effectiveness cannot be greater than your ability to make the right decisions. When we look at the success stories of great leaders, we see that the difference between them and ordinary people lies in the decisions they made at critical junctures in their lives. Those decisions became a watershed moment that defined them and propelled them to greatness.

Can you write the history of the civil rights movement in the United States without the decision of Rosa Parks not to give up her seat or the decision of Martin Luther King Jr. to quit his pastorate and lend his voice to the movement? Decisions create leaders out of ordinary men and women and propel them into life's Hall of Fame.

They Are Afraid of Making a Mistake

While the fear of making a mistake is a legitimate fear, great leaders do not allow it to prevent them from making crucial decisions because failure to do so is a major mistake in itself. I have good news for you: You will never have a perfect record in decision making! You will always make mistakes. The most important thing is to learn from the mistakes and move on. Even some of your so-called best decisions will end in disaster. Are they then a reason to crucify yourself? Absolutely not. If a decision you made in the best interest of the organization did not go well, learn from it and move on.

I like Abraham Lincoln's mindset when he said in his speech to the subtreasury in 1839, "The probability that we may fall in the struggle ought not to deter us from the support of a cause we believe to be just; it shall not deter me."[7] Refuse to let the fear of failure hold you back. Stories abound of leaders who—because they were afraid of making a mistake—allowed market share to slip and were eventually sacked.

Decisions: The Strength of Leadership

Leadership comes wrapped in decision-making responsibilities. Leadership is a choice we make, not a title we have or a space we occupy or a place where we sit in the organization. Through decisions we steer the ship of our personal and organizational lives in the direction we want. Therefore, the ability to make the right decisions is the defining hallmark of a great leader. Strategy boils down to decisions, so does innovation and customer service. Everything in leadership can be summarized as a set of decisions. Your attitude is a decision, so is engagement of staff. Organizational failure also boils down to decisions—wrong decisions in strategy, people, or execution. So, I'd say that *the primary responsibility of a leader is to make the decisions that secure the future of the organization.* Think about it: Leaders who fail to make the right decisions end up destroying thousands of lives. Think of the thousands who lost their jobs in the subprime mortgage crisis in the United States and the subsequent stock market crash and global recession. The destruction that a leader leaves in the wake of a poor decision can sometimes be monumental.

Nature of Decisions

Decisions can be classified in many ways, but here are five simple ways to look at decisions:

- *Focus*: task focused or people focused
- *Occurrence*: first time or routine
- *Duration*: long term or short term
- *Importance*: strategic or operational/tactical
- *Impact*: Significant or minor

For example, the decision to send a man to the moon and return him safely to earth by John F. Kennedy can be classified as task focused, first time, long term, strategic, and significant. You get the idea.

Task-focused decisions deal with your strategic intent and the work at hand. Any decision that focuses on the results aspect of the leadership equation is usually task focused, while those that focus on the relationships aspect are people focused. People-focused decisions are usually more difficult to make because of the emotional aspect involved. For example, should you fire a poor performer who has been in the company for 10 years?

Effective leaders know how to balance task-focused decisions with people-focused decisions—they balance the tough skin with a tender heart. For example, poor performance is always both a task-related and people-related issue. Poor performance could result from a combination of any of these factors: A lack of clarity about the task (task focused), the absence of resources to accomplish the task (task focused), inadequate skill set on the part of the worker (both task and people focused), or even a lack of motivation (people focused).

The debate has been raging for decades: Should leaders focus on tasks or people? I believe they should do both. Leadership is achieving results (task focused) through people (people focused). Focusing only on one aspect of our leadership equation will not achieve the desired results. However, decisions that need to be made should be made even if some might be hurt. To allow emotions becloud your sense of judgment is a recipe for leadership failure.

I believe the task aspect of a leader's decision making can be subdivided into two: operational and strategic.

- *Operational tasks* are inward looking and deal with the optimization of current processes or with tactical problems like the resolution of customer complaints. They are more administrative in nature.
- *Strategic tasks* are usually significant in impact and long in duration (medium to long term in nature and affect the nature of operations to engage in, the products to launch, the businesses to start, the market segments to enter, and so on). They are more innovative in nature.

A leader must balance both types of tasks effectively. To focus on administrative tasks without innovation will make the organization a success story today but a relic of yesterday's history tomorrow. But to focus on innovation alone without administration means that the organization will become a blighted ovum—an organization that did not live to see the rewards of its efforts. A leader must focus on both. She must have one foot planted in the present (administration) and another in the future (innovation).

When a company has burgeoning costs and can't meet deadlines and targets, the most important decision required is administrative—to fix today's issues. While administrative decisions will fix today's problems, they will not capture tomorrow's opportunities. So, leaders must focus on the opportunities to innovate in order to secure the future of the organization.

Routine decisions should not be brought to the attention of the leader. The leader should provide policy guidelines where people know what to do and the decisions to take in routine situations.

Decision-Making Guide

- *Define the problem.* What are the symptoms?
  - Task focused, people focused, or a combination of both?
  - First time or reoccurrence?
  - Significant or minor?
- *Pinpoint the root cause.* Perform a root-cause analysis. Never start brainstorming for solutions without first identifying the root cause of the problem. What exactly is the cause of the problem here? Without identifying the root cause, you will only be treating the symptoms.
- *Develop criteria for the plan.* What will the possible solution satisfy? For example, we decided to move the location of our organization. Before deciding where to move, we listed the criteria that the new place should satisfy. One of the conditions for the new location was price; others included parking space, safe environment, and accessibility for the key workforce. The conditions helped people not just to think outside the box in a wild goose chase but also think within the box, given the criteria that the solution must satisfy.
- *Brainstorm possible solutions.* Give people a free rein to use their imaginations to list possible solutions. At this stage, no idea is stupid. Just list them. After you have finished listing them, use your criteria to test the options and see which meets the test.

- *Determine the best solution.* After brainstorming and using the criteria to evaluate them, it is time to make the decision. The best solution is the one that addresses the root cause of the problem. At this stage, avoid being too emotional and being too considerate. No decision will satisfy all your constituents. Choose the best decision for the good of the organization. Leaders give away their power when they wait until they can make a decision every person in the team is happy with.
- *Act on the decision.* Peter F. Drucker once said that a decision is not a decision unless it has some form of action built into it. It might be a suggestion, an opinion, a thought, and so on, but a decision must have an action plan built into it. So what next after you have made the decision?
- *Build flexibility into decisions.* No matter how perfect a decision may be, there are unforeseen circumstances that might necessitate a review of the decision. Review the decision and learn from it. If there is difficulty with the implementation or the implementation is not yielding the desired results, it's time to review the decision and begin the process again.

Three Quick Reminders before Deciding

Whatever the nature of the decision you want to make, here are my three guiding rules:

1. **Ensure that you gather sufficient information and involve key people**

   Never rush to a decision without gathering relevant and sufficient information. Don't operate *leadership by gossip as a management style.* Also, before making decisions, please ensure that you involve the key people.

2. **Ensure that the decision is in the best interest of your organization and is fair to all**

   Don't take a decision just to satisfy a powerful few at the expense of the greater majority. As a leader, you must be seen to be fair to all. Nothing erodes your leadership effectiveness faster than a lack of transparency, favoritism and nepotism.

3. **Think through the potential impact of the decision**

   Often, leaders make decisions without thinking through the impact of such decisions. Driven by a sense of urgency, they commit to a course of action that will destroy the future of the organization. If there is anything you will take out of the concept of decision-making, it is this: Every decision carries with it the seed of a future consequence. Decisions have ripple effects. Once made, they reverberate and amplify throughout the organization over time. Nothing erodes your leadership faster than making decisions your people feel are stupid or not well thought through. If they cannot trust your ability to make the right decisions in simple matters, how can they trust your leadership ability in critical situations? Admitting that you did not think through the unintended consequences is an attribute of a poor leader. Don't make that mistake. Think it through.

Credibility versus Popularity

To become decisive, a leader must question his motive. What is the driving force—to win popularity or build credibility? I believe that leadership is not a friendship or popularity contest. Leadership sometimes entails personal risk—to do what you feel is right and in the long-term interests of your constituents even when such decisions are unpopular in the short term. Leaders must wrestle with and accept the fact that they might not be popular in the short run when they take some tough decisions. Some people will be disappointed; others will simply walk away; and still others may protest. However, in the long run, leaders will win the admiration of their people and even their critics if they act in the overall best interests of their organizations and constituents. Leaders who sacrifice credibility at the altar of popularity end up destroying their leadership capability. Don't become such a leader.

Jessica—A Very Loyal Staff

Jessica is a very loyal staff of the organization. She has been with the organization for 10 years, during which time you have become very good friends, although you are her boss. The first 6 years, she was very productive. However, she has been below average in her performance in the last 4 years. The main reason is partly her inability to adapt to the changes happening in the business environment and upgrade her skills.

You decided to put her on a performance improvement plan, but you realized after 18 months that her capacity will not meet the new challenges. It is not a motivation problem but a capacity problem.

You have seen an A-rated performer in another organization and she is willing to join you. She has another offer but will give up that for your organization if you can make a counter offer. You have requested for the management's approval to employ her, but the management has requested that you replace one person in your team with the new staff.

Jessica is currently the lowest performer in the team. To employ the new staff, you will have to let her go but you know, in confidence, that her child is having some medical challenges and she is a single mother. f you let her go, the child's health will suffer. If you don't, you cannot employ the new staff and the department might continue to struggle. What would you do?

My Commitment

"I commit to being a decisive leader."

Now go ahead and write specific ways to achieve the commitment you've made.

1. _____
2. _____
3. _____

CHAPTER 4

Love What You Do, Whom You Do It with, and Whom You Do It for

The saddest people I've ever met in life are the ones who don't care deeply about anything at all. Passion and satisfaction go hand in hand, and without them, any happiness is only temporary, because there's nothing to make it last.

—Nicholas Sparks, *Dear John*

Ever wonder what's the greatest leadership secret of all time? Wonder no more. It is this:

There are no great leaders, only great principles.

This is perhaps the greatest leadership secret I have discovered from my years of research on the topic of leadership. The more I study leadership, the more I am amazed at the simple fact that there are no great leaders, only great principles. I know you will be surprised at the simplicity of what I call the greatest leadership secret of all time and wonder how this secret holds the key to unlocking your own leadership effectiveness.

Each time I mention the greatest leadership secret in my seminars, my audiences are surprised and shocked, to say the least. If there are no great leaders, what about the exploits of men and women like Abraham Lincoln, Thomas Edison, Susanna Wesley, Golda Meir, and Steve Jobs, for example?

Great leaders are simply ordinary people who built their lives around great principles.

A closer look at the lives of these great men and women reveals that the commonality of their greatness is the application of principles despite the differences in race, gender, geographical location, dispensations, religious inclinations, and educational qualifications.

Abraham Lincoln's Emancipation Proclamation was founded on the principle of the equality of all men. This conviction produced one of the greatest presidents the United States has ever had. The same principle revealed Martin Luther King Jr. as a great leader. Winston Churchill preserved his name among the great because of the principles of perseverance and the sovereignty of all nations; Mother Teresa, the principle of compassion for the less privileged.

Permit me to repeat again: There are no great leaders, only great principles. While their personalities, leadership styles, and religious inclinations might have been different, they became great because they chose to apply certain principles of success and leadership. The context of the expression of the principles might have been shaped by their gender, environment, challenges, and education, but one thing is common: They achieved greatness by their unalloyed allegiance and obedience to principles.

The beauty of principles is that they do not respect gender, race or geographies, and as such, we all can be great by applying the principles of leadership. A closer look at different leaders reveals that there is one principle or quality that is the sine qua non of leadership greatness. This quality is important for success in life, but more importantly, for leadership, and it separates great leaders from ordinary ones. Great leaders have a high dose of this quality, while ordinary leaders lack it. Without this quality, achieving leadership greatness or improving your leadership effectiveness is a mirage.

What is this quality? I'd say it is *love or passion.* Great leaders are passionate people. Passion is the fire that keeps them going from one height of greatness to another. Passion wakes them up in the morning and keeps them awake all night. Passion infuses extra energy into them and propels them all the way. Passion makes them sacrifice life's luxuries just to build a great or successful life or a great institution. Without passion, leadership effectiveness is a daydream.

Look at the history of any great leader, and you find the common thread of passion and the willingness to sacrifice their very existence for their dreams. Louis Gerstner, the man who saved IBM from bankruptcy, observed in his book *Who Says Elephants Can't Dance? Inside IBM's Historic Turnaround*, "Great institutions are not managed; they are led. They are not administered; they are driven to ever-increasing levels of accomplishment by individuals who are passionate about winning."

Passion for winning is the driving force of leadership greatness. Show me any great leader, and I will show you someone who is passionate about something worthwhile—whatever that thing is. Generally, taking a cue from corporate leadership, a great leader's passion can be divided into three:

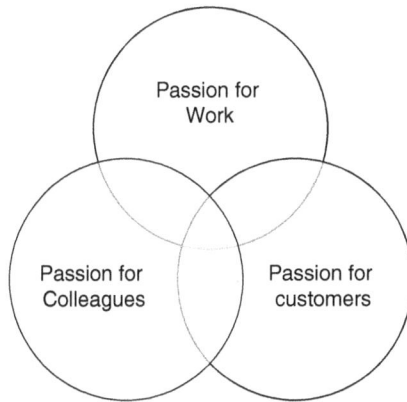

Passion for Work: Love What You Do

Leadership greatness without loving what you do is impossible. Why? Because work is the womb of greatness. Nobody ever achieved greatness outside the realm of work—whatever that work is (whether it is singing, playing football, building a business, or leading a team). But without passion, work becomes a chore and leads to boredom. People achieve greatness when they so love what they do that they are willing to do it for free, even though they are often paid for doing it.

> Until your work becomes an avenue to express your life's calling and gifts, you will never achieve true greatness.

Work for such individuals is not just the means of earning a livelihood but also the means of creating the life they've always wanted. Work, for them, is the channel for the expression of their life's callings and gifts.

Perhaps the best advice on passion for work was given by Steve Jobs at the commencement address at Stanford University in 2005, when he said,

> You've got to find what you love. And that is as true for your work as it is for your lovers. Your work is going to fill a large part of your life, and the only way to be truly satisfied is to do what you believe is great work. And the only way to do great work is to love what you do.[8]

I like the notion that "the only way to do great work is to love what you do." Because great leaders love what they do, they achieve greatness. Love or passion for work usually precedes greatness. Show me someone who loves what he does and is willing to sacrifice his time and resources to be the best at it, and I will show you someone who will achieve greatness in that field.

Passion for Colleagues and Customers: Love Whom You Do It with and Do It For

While much has been said and written about passion for work and results, I think most leadership literatures miss the focus of the passion of great leaders. It is not just about passion for work and results but also passion for people—whom they work with, and more importantly, whom they work for. For great leaders, people are not a stepping stone to achieving personal results or building a personal kingdom. People are not a means to an end but the end of their means.

The premise of this book is that leadership is "relationships × results," and different chapters deal with a leader's relationship with his people. So, I'd like to focus on the third aspect of a leader's passion, which is in fact the focus of great leaders' passion—the end users or whom they work for. Whether corporate or religious leadership, we all have end users of our products and services. When I talk about whom you work for, I am not referring to the organization you work for but to the end users of your products and services: your customers. You work in an organization, but you actually work for your customers. Don't confuse where you work with whom you work for. Without customers, organizations do not exist. Organizations do not exist just for shareholders; they also exist for their customers. Ask People Express's founders.

Great leaders are passionate about their customers. They are driven by the plight of the human condition, the injustice in society, the cruelty of the oppression of the poor, and the exploitation of end users as a result of corporate greed. Their passion to make a difference stems from being in touch with the pains and tears and sufferings of the average person. As it were, they become social crusaders, using their resources to achieve results, better-quality results, for their constituents and their customers.

I'd say that while great leaders love what they do, more importantly, they love whom they do it for. Without loving those you work for, you cannot climb the stairs of leadership greatness. Your results will not be sustainable. That is, passion for results, while it is good, can self-destruct if it is not yoked with passion for people. Passion for results must be yoked with compassion for people. A leader with a passion only for results will be like a bull without restraint—aggressive and destructive. It will be the equivalent of ambition without the right attitude.

Most great leaders yoke their passion for results with their love for people. Without passion for people, passion for results can become self-seeking, mean, and ruthless. Great work is seen in satisfied customers. The joy in the end users' faces is the passion that drives great leaders to do great work.

I came to this realization in 2006 when I was saddled with the responsibility of leading a disgruntled group that had experienced many changes in leadership prior to my arrival. Although I'd held various leadership positions prior to this one, the new task was one I wasn't really prepared for. With changing leadership, the members of the group no longer felt important. Productivity was abysmal. Morale was low, and so was the attendance. Some members of the group left the organization as they did not want to have anything to do with another leader sent from the headquarters who they were not sure would be with them till the end.

Our first meeting was one I can never forget. The members were trying to size me up. Would I be the kind of leader that they would want to work with? Could I be trusted? Would it be worth their while? I understood their pains. Having faced leaders in the past who made promises but couldn't keep them can be emotionally traumatic. Their past leaders had failed them. The confidence they reposed in their former leaders had been shattered. Their trust had been betrayed. The emotional turmoil of the past made it difficult to believe in the possibilities of the future.

It was in this kind of situation I found myself. All my awards for exemplary leadership didn't make any sense to me. I wondered after the first meeting why I had accepted the challenge. I wanted to quit to preserve my past records, but somehow, I couldn't. I felt their pain so much that I didn't want to add to it.

And since I promised not to be like their former leaders who had failed them, I was morally obligated to serve out my tenure with them.

I learned two pivotal lessons of leadership while working with the group. The first is as follows:

People, not fame and success, are the reason for leadership.

When I accepted the challenge to lead the group, I did so because I wanted the organization to know that I was a great leader. I wanted to succeed not because I really cared about the people, but I saw the challenge as an opportunity to improve my curriculum vitae and move ahead in life. The group was just a stepping stone to my personal gain. The people were not really important to me.

However, after seeing the pain in their eyes and working with them for months, my motives changed. I wanted to make a personal difference in their lives more than I wanted to achieve success. If success meant putting hope back into the lives of a disgruntled group, if it meant rekindling the passion for the future, if it meant making them believe that they could still achieve something worthwhile with their lives, then I wanted to be a success because of them.

The fame and honor no longer mattered to me. My reputation no longer mattered. I came to love the group and strove to be the kind of leader that they would be proud of. Now my definition of success was wrapped around making a difference in their lives.

The second lesson I learned is as follows:

A leader must love his people to serve them effectively.

Without loving people, a leader will use them to achieve his aims. Without loving people, a leader will not make the necessary sacrifices to help them succeed even if it means going to the cross for them. It is love that binds a leader to his followers. It is love that makes a leader devote his time to coach his team. It is love that causes a leader to challenge them to be their best. It is love that stimulates innovation and produces great products. Love for people is the harbinger for passion for great results. Great leaders love what they do, but they love more whom they do it with. They love people the way they met them but love them too much to leave them that way!

So, do you love the people you work with and the end users you work for? Do you love them enough to give your life in exchange for their wellbeing? To give up your personal gain for their good? To sacrifice your welfare for their advantage? To put them first? That's the secret of leadership greatness, to love your people so much that you are willing to sacrifice your personal comfort for their wellbeing and future.

My Commitment

"I commit to loving what I do, whom I do it with, and whom I do it for."

Now go ahead and write specific ways to achieve the commitment you've made.

1. _____
2. _____
3. _____

CHAPTER 5

Service-Oriented Leadership

The first responsibility of a leader is to define reality. The last is to say thank you. In between the two, the leader must become a servant and a debtor. That sums up the progress of an artful leader.

—Max De Pree

Leadership is spelt S-E-R-V-I-C-E. The call to leadership is a call to serve. If there is one central truth about leadership, it is this: A leader's greatness is directly proportional to his ability to serve. The more he serves his people, the more he is served by his constituents and customers. Therefore, leaders, real leaders, adopt the mindset of "the one that serves" and not that of "the one that rules." Like a waiter in a restaurant whose motto is "At your service," a leader is supposed to be at the service of his people. Real leaders wait on their people, serving their needs. They understand that positions are simply the platforms or the opportunities and privileges given to them to serve their people. And they do so gladly!

Great leaders are not afraid of serving their people. The truth is, they earn their place in history because of their sacrificial spirit and attitude. Agnes Gonxha Bojaxhiu (Mother Teresa) is a classic example. Leaders who are afraid that stooping to serve their people will make them lose the respect of their people are insecure leaders and always end up as dictators. Great leaders, because they are secure in themselves, know that little acts like washing their disciples' feet, following Jesus's example, do not belittle them.

So how do leaders serve their people? Here's a SERVICE acronym to show you how leaders serve.

S—Simplicity

When great leaders are with their followers, they appear ordinary. This is perhaps one of the greatest principles of effective leadership. While outsiders are impressed with the charisma and personality of the leader, to their followers, leaders are just as human as any other person. They have no air of superiority about them. They do not see themselves any more special than their followers because of the positions they occupy.

I believe people who are conscious of titles and positions do not have anything else to offer. When we hold dearly to our titles, it means there is nothing else to our persons. Because true leaders know that the position doesn't make them, they don't emphasize their positions/titles in dealing with their people. As best-selling leadership author, John Maxwell, rightly noted, "Insecure leaders are into titles; secure leaders, into towels."

One manifestation of simplicity is accessibility and being easy to relate to. These leaders can be reached. Today, I see leaders who are not accessible, who are not in touch with the realities of the needs of their people, who make their people feel that they are too busy to attend to them, who cannot stoop to wash their people's feet—and I shudder! Why? Great leaders break down the communication barriers between them and their people. What is the opposite of simplicity? Complexity (i.e., difficult to deal with). When followers find it difficult to relate to a leader, then that leader has guaranteed that his impact on his followers will be limited.

When we fail to serve our people, we miss the purpose of our leadership calling. We can impress people from a distance, but we cannot make any positive impact until we identify with our people and serve their needs.

E—Example

Great leaders lead by example. They roll up their sleeves and demonstrate what needs to be done. They know that education is not taught, it is caught (that is, people learn faster through models than through lectures). They know that the best way of teaching people is not by sermonizing but by modeling the behaviors they expect from their followers. The verdict is out: A leader has no moral justification to expect from his followers what he himself is not willing to do. Thus, he cannot lead his people further than he has traveled in his own personal experiences. Why? Followers usually rise to the level of the leader's lifestyles and not his teachings.

Leaders lead by example. Your *right to lead* is directly proportional to your *willingness to serve*. Your right to teach is tied to your personal testimonies as the best messages are not preached—they are lived and demonstrated! People understand your instructions through your lifestyle. They learn the organizational values through your virtues. Model it, and they will imitate you. Teach me, and I may forget it, but demonstrate it, and I will never forget it.

R—Relevance

Relevance means leaders make their world a better place. They leave their generations with inspiring testimonies, touch the lives of others in a personal way, and leave their thumbprints indelibly upon the hearts of their fellow citizens. They are like the salt of the earth and the light of their world. When a leader is relevant, his absence can be felt because of the contributions his presence makes. They are individuals who have so developed themselves that they become, as it were, *indispensable* to their organizations. Some might argue that no one is truly indispensable; however, true leaders are not easily replaceable. When you are relevant, people miss your absence.

In an organizational setting, relevance is the essence of strategy. Most organizations do not know why they exist or have forgotten the reason for their existence. Somehow, along the course of "normal business," they have lost their organizational essence.

Regaining your organizational essence begins with recapturing the MVP (mission, vision, and purpose) statements of the organization. A closer look at most organizations' MVP statements reveals their organizational essence—to be relevant to a particular segment of a served market. Simply put, organizations exist because of their relevance to customers, and organizational success is determined by how relevant these organizations continually remain to customers' needs.

If customers are the reason for organizational existence, what is the goal of leading organizations? *Surprised clients!* Leading organizations are one step ahead of customers' needs and expectations. The people, systems, and processes are geared toward ensuring that customers' expectations are continually exceeded. As Gary Hamel and C.K. Prahalad noted in *Competing for the Future*, leading organizations "fundamentally reinvent existing competitive space or invent entirely new competitive space in ways that amaze customers and dismay competitors."

Leading organizations go beyond satisfying their clients; they surprise them!

Surprised clients are an organization's best advertisement. Why? When customers are pleasantly surprised at the quality of your service delivery, when your service/product completely exceeds their wildest imaginations, they become your organization's ambassadors and begin to market your services to other clients. Therefore, the best strategies, processes, structures, and systems within organizations are the ones geared toward ensuring that customers' expectations are exceeded. When systems, processes, and structures stifle excellent customer service delivery, that organization has guaranteed that its demise is near.

V—Value

Leaders add value to their people. In fact, the essence of leadership is about value creation in people, customers and organizations. The more value you add to people, the more you are celebrated as a leader. Think leadership? Think value creation. More on this in Section 3.

I—Integrity

Leaders serve with integrity. So important is integrity to service and leadership that we have already touched on it and will further address it in chapter 13 that is dedicated to trust.

C—Compassionate

Leaders serve because they are compassionate people. They are moved by the plight of their people. Passion and compassion go together (see Chapter 4). Compassionate people are in touch with their own feelings and the feelings of others. They connect with the challenges of their people and look for ways to help them—what has been termed *empathy*. Just as the skeletal system holds the human body in place and the heart pumps blood for strength, *compassion* is both the skeletal system and the heart of real service. Why would leaders go the extra mile to render exceptional service? Compassion. Why do some lawyers take up cases of poor clients who cannot afford to pay them and represent them in court? Compassion.

Compassion is just showing that you care. You care enough to ask about your team's challenges, welfare, and future aspirations. Compassion is not about developing the messianic complex, thinking you must solve all your team's or organizational problems. It is being concerned enough about your people to notice subtle changes about them and doing what you can, within the limits of your abilities, to alleviate their pain and suffering.

E—Enthusiastic

Leaders serve enthusiastically. They look forward to serving. They enjoy it. Because they know that service is the rite of passage to leadership greatness, they serve with a smile and are excited every time they see a customer or their people coming with a request. Their understanding of the importance of service is the fuel that keeps them going with enthusiasm. Without this understanding, enthusiasm is impossible. They know that *serving people's needs is life's gateway to greatness.* Their enthusiasm manifests in three ways:

- *Speed:* Because they are enthusiastic, they are filled with energy. They do not drag their feet to serve customers or employees. They are prompt. They are responsive. They watch their turnaround time.
- *Respect:* Because they love their customers, they are polite in their manner of approach, words, and behaviors. They do not argue with the customers or shout at their staff. They do not complain or moan or serve grudgingly.
- *Excellence:* Because they are excited about what they do, they keep pushing the envelope of performance. They do not rest on their

laurels. They are not satisfied with yesterday's best. They adopt the Japanese philosophy of *kaizen,* continuous improvement with respect to their services to their clients. They constantly experiment and innovate to explore new ways of doing old things. They keep surprising their clients. The *wow* factor on the faces of their customers and employees is not a one-time occurrence for them but a daily occurrence. They serve with a string of excellent products.

As you go about your roles this week, don't ever forget that a true leader waits on his people. Adopt the motto "At your service" and watch your leadership potential grow. Be secure in your person. Little acts do not belittle you. Look around you; there are always little acts of service to render to your world. Don't debate whose job it is; just do it.

My Commitment

"I commit to serving my people."

Now go ahead and write specific ways to achieve the commitment you've made.

1. _____
2. _____
3. _____

CHAPTER 6

How Will You Be Remembered?

Real leaders do not sacrifice their most important relationships—family, friends, colleagues—to achieve results.

What do you want the world to remember about you? What would your team members remember you for? Sometimes, leaders forget that every position is transient and just as their rise to power has a start date it also has an end date. The difference between great leaders and mediocre ones is simple: Great leaders know that there is an end date and want to make a significant difference before their end date arrives while mediocre leaders lose sight of the end date thinking their position is eternal.

Think of the following executives:

- Al "Chainsaw" Dunlap of Sunbeam Products who compared himself to "Rambo in Pinstripes" and who was disgraced out of office and barred from serving in a publicly quoted company for the accounting scandals he committed at Sunbeam.[9]
- Gerald Levin who destroyed shareholders' funds of over $200bn as CEO of Time Warner in his infamous merger with AOL and is listed as one of the worst CEOs of all time by CNBC.com[10].

I ask again: How will you be remembered? Or what do you want them to remember about you?

As we come to the end of the person of the leader section, you need to realize that great leaders are zealous about their legacy. So, what will your legacy be? At the heart of your legacy is the desire to leave your organization and people better off, to not destroy value.

To help you get started, here are four pillars to consider:

- Live with the greater good in mind
- Be true to your values
- Redefine what success means for you
- Plan for successors

Live with the Greater Good in Mind

There is a direct relationship between your leadership influence and your personal beliefs and obedience to the concept of the greater good. Think of great leaders, and you will see that they transcended selfishness to selflessness.

They gave themselves away for the good of their generations. In my book *The Difference: What Successful People Know and Do That Ordinary People Do Not*, I wrote,

> The concept of "the greater good," whether explicitly written or not, is one that differentiates successful people from ordinary people, successful leaders from ordinary leaders. Successful individuals and companies lived and abided by the code "for the greater good." Ordinary individuals lived for themselves, and, themselves only. If corporate executives like Ken Lay and Jeffrey Skilling of Enron, Bernie Ebbers of WorldCom, Dennis Kozlowski of Tyco, Bernard "Bernie" Madoff of the famed Madoff Ponzi scheme, and corporate turnaround specialist and downsizer Al Dunlap had lived by the code "for the greater good" perhaps they wouldn't have gone down history with such ignominy that their names are associated with.

Be True to Your Values

Your values are your personal compass. Just as organizations have corporate values that determine their behaviors and give them a sense of identity, your values are your unique identity in an overcrowded and confused world. Achieving greatness as a leader without some alignment with your values is a mirage.

Most times, when I teach about values, I ask the participants the following questions:

Me: *What is guilt?*
Them: *It's feeling bad about something.*
Me: *Why do you feel bad about it?*
Them: *Because you know it's bad.*
Me: *How do you know that it's bad, or who told you that it's bad?*
Them: *You just know it.*
Me: *How?*

We keep going back and forth until the light dawns on them that they have a set of values (whether conscious or not) and every action is weighed from the perspective of their values. I define *guilt* as the gap between one's actions and one's values. Your values are not just a guide to aid you in making decisions but also the umpire to judge your actions. When your actions align with your values, you derive a measure of joy and satisfaction, but when they don't, you feel bad or guilty. As a leader, without resolving the gap between your values and your actions, your success will be temporary, and you will not derive satisfaction from external achievements that are not in sync with your values.

Leaders live from their sense of personal values. They know what is important to them beyond making money, and they ensure that when they reach the end of their lives, they can look back with the feeling of satisfaction that they have lived life to the fullest and in concert with their values. They do not allow external pressures to govern their behavioral responses. I am yet to see anyone who achieved lasting leadership greatness without being clear of the things that are important to him and living his life every day in line with them. If you don't structure your day to ensure that your behaviors align with your values, you will not achieve true and lasting leadership greatness.

Redefine What Success Means to You

Just as important as knowing and living life from your values, leadership success happens when we define what success means to you.

Permit me to quote again from *The Difference*. . .

For me, success is finishing strong. Life's finest honors are given at the end of the race. While the world might applaud because of the score at halftime, Life waits till the end to give out its honors.

Finishing strong is also finishing with your moral virtues and dignity intact. Who wants to associate with individuals who achieved success at the expense of their moral virtues? Moral bankruptcies are far more dangerous than financial bankruptcies. Ask the partners of Arthur Andersen. The age-long advice, "What shall it profit a man if he gains the whole world at the expense of his soul?" still holds true for successful people.

So, my friend, this for me is success, and, I hope for you also.

To be happy with yourself and your contributions to humanity.

To know that you did not lose your virtues in the pursuit of your victories.

You did not sacrifice your most important relationships—family, friends, colleagues—to achieve your results.

Your kids are proud to have you as a parent, your spouse as a partner, your friends as their buddy, and your colleagues and subordinates proud to have worked with you.

You lived your life without any regrets because you are at peace upwards with your maker, inward with yourself and outward with your society.

You died empty for your life was poured out in libation until every gift was maximised, every talent harnessed, and every potential achieved for the benefit of humanity and the glory of divinity.

That someone somewhere might not have succeeded without your contribution in their life.

Somebody, somewhere, someday will say, "Thank God you were born and you truly lived!"

So, if you can look forward with hope because you are happy with the future, around with confidence because you are happy with your relationships, backward with satisfaction because you are happy with your contributions to humanity and inward with pride because you are happy with yourself and the life you've lived, then, you are a success!

Plan for Successors

It doesn't matter what you achieve as a leader; if you hand over to the wrong person or do not plan your transition very well, all your successes will be short lived. Ask Howard Schultz of Starbucks. Your goal must be to build something—whatever that thing is—to succeed without you, something enduring and lasting. And to do that, you need to plan for your successors well in advance of your retirement. Planning for successors involves the following steps:

- *Know when to leave:* Blessed is the leader who knows when to take a bow and leave the stage for the next generation. Look at the African continent, and you will agree with me that most African leaders do not know when to leave, and their refusal to leave has held the continent backward. When a leader stays longer than is necessary, he actually destroys value. Know when to leave.
- *Begin the search early:* Don't start the search the year you are supposed to leave. Start earlier. Getting the right successor usually takes time. Follow the advice of founder and former CEO of Visa Inc., Dee Hock:

  Hire and promote first on the basis of integrity; second, motivation; third, capacity; fourth, understanding; fifth, knowledge; and last and least, experience. Without integrity, motivation is dangerous; without motivation, capacity is impotent; without capacity, understanding is limited; without understanding, knowledge is meaningless; without knowledge, experience is blind. Experience is easy to provide and quickly put to good use by people with all the other qualities.[11]

- *Mentor appropriately:* Make the transition seamless by instituting an apprenticeship scheme for the new leader. Leaders who don't mentor appropriately would see their successes destroyed by the new leader. Time spent getting the new leader up to speed and providing direction is time well spent.
- *Look forward, not backward.* Once you have handed over and mentored appropriately, then it's time to allow the new leader to run the affairs of the company. If you still have to control all the decisions, then you either did not select the right person or did not mentor appropriately or perhaps you are suffering from personal insecurity. It's time to look forward. Move on to the next big thing in your life. I wish you well!

SECTION 2

Inspire and Influence Your Team

This segment is about inspiring hope and confidence in your people. The first section has laid the foundation for this segment. For example, you cannot inspire people if your attitude is wrong or you are perceived as someone without integrity. Having laid the foundation, leaders must inspire and influence people to buy into their visions and develop the confidence in their team to execute the project.

Great leaders inspire hope and confidence. They show us what is possible and push us to accomplish it. Call them optimists, possibility thinkers, visionaries, or idealists—they are individuals who are willing to challenge the status quo to find new and better ways of doing old things.

I believe one of the most important tasks of organizational leadership is to breathe life and vitality into organizations, to awaken the spirit of possibility, creativity, and innovation in them. And breathing life and vitality is best done through inspiring hope and confidence.

Inspiring hope is all about the future. But leaders do much more than just to inspire hope; they inspire confidence in the present. Inspiring hope without inspiring confidence is a daydream, an unrealistic Pollyannaish attitude toward life. Inspiring confidence is the belief that your future is possible and is done by communicating your faith in your people's ability to bring that vision to pass.

Dreams die where confidence is lacking, and it is the leader's responsibility to develop the confidence of his team. Bold dreams require bold steps. And bold steps are impossible without confidence and courage. Without inspiring confidence in your team, they will settle for mediocrity and be happy about it.

This section will cover the following five topics:

- Bold dreams
- Grow your people
- Engage your constituents
- Motivate your employees
- Unify constituents around a common cause

CHAPTER 7

Bold Dreams

People who are crazy enough to think they can change the world are the ones who do.

—Steve Jobs

The world is a better place today because of ordinary men and women who dared to dream. Had it not been for the dreams of these men and women, humanity would have remained in caves. It was a dream that gave us space travel, television, heart surgery, and telephones; placed a man on the moon; harnessed the energies of the sun; and conquered diseases that long held sway over the human race. A dream gave birth to the world you and I are living in, and dreams make it a better place every day. Even the book you are reading now is the product of a dream.

When we think of great leaders, the common thread in the tapestry of their leadership greatness is the ability to dream a bold new dream. Some call it a dream; others call it burning desire, aspiration, audacious goal, or vision. What name you use is irrelevant; the concept is the same—the willingness to dream and to dream big, to envision future possibilities yet unseen by others, to dare the seemingly impossible in order to create a new future. And you can tell a leader by the size of his dreams as dreams are the foundation upon which the house of leadership is built.

Leaders dream big. Invariably, it's the size of their dreams that makes them achieve greatness and enter the Hall of Fame. When Martin Luther King Jr. stood on the steps of the Lincoln Memorial on August 28, 1963 and delivered his famous "I Have a Dream" speech, he was demonstrating this attribute of leadership. The dream was big and bold. It was inspiring and challenging. It was unique and different. It created a movement. It looked impossible then, but Barack Obama's position as the 44th president of the United States is a reflection of King's dream and a testament that dreams do come true. When President J.F. Kennedy on May 25, 1961, as part of his State of the Union Address challenged Congress and indeed all Americans to send a man to the moon and return him safely to earth, it looked impossible. But on July 20, 1969, Neil Armstrong became the first man to walk on the moon.

Leadership is impossible without dreams. If leadership is relationships × results, then leaders cannot lead effectively without clarifying the results that they want. And since results are usually futuristic—something outside the present—leadership must begin with a clear vision of the end result that is sought. Without clarity of the end goal you seek, how will you motivate or inspire people toward accomplishing it? Therefore, leadership begins with *dreams.*

If the dream is exciting, the leader will find a way to mobilize the people and resources he needs and figure out a way to get there. Is it not interesting to note that Luther did not say "I have a plan"? Over 250,000 people would not have gathered to hear his plans! While plans are necessary for dreams to become realities, plans hold no fire to stimulate the hearts of men. The hearts of men are stirred up and set on fire by bold dreams—a challenge to incumbency, a break from the status quo, and an invitation to greatness for ordinary folks. People are looking to join causes that will outlive them, to do something significant with their lives, to live an extraordinary life, and only bold dreams will fulfill their quest and awaken the slumbering spirit of achievement resident inside them.

> Dreams give meaning to life. They are the compass of life's journey, the backbone of great achievements.

Without a bold dream, people and organizations settle for mediocrity. Without a bold dream that inspires them, people become selfish and self-centered. Without a bold dream calling them to step out of the known into the future to chart new territories, break new grounds, or pioneer new inventions, people will be satisfied with playing second fiddle and justifying it.

When Steve Jobs returned to Apple Inc. in 1997, the company was on the verge of bankruptcy. It was his bold dream to give power to the designers for them to design products that customers would love that became the rallying cry within the company and enlivened the spirit of creativity and innovation that turned the company into the powerhouse that it is today. His bold dream or vision not only challenged the incumbents but also challenged the slumbering spirit within Apple Inc. to rise to the occasion and create masterpieces for the world to copy. Leadership is truly impossible without bold dreams.

Bold Dreams Defined

In my leadership seminars and training sessions, I am tempted to reduce things to simple concepts (like the 4Ps) and even formulas (like relationships $\times$ results) and acronyms (like IDEAL or SERVICE) to help people remember them. Without being simplistic or formulaic, I will attempt to define a bold dream as the relationship between opportunities (current and future) and current organizational resources and capabilities.

In a formula, it will appear as follows:

$$\text{Bold dreams} = \frac{\text{Opportunities (current + future)}}{\text{Current organizational resources and capabilities}}$$

Current Opportunities

A dream is simply the recognition of an opportunity, both current and future. Sometimes a bold dream happens simply by looking at your current situation differently and asking, Is there a better way of delivering existing products and services? Is there a market segment being overlooked by current offerings?

Leaders must constantly ask themselves if opportunities exist right now in their current business or customer segments or what some business leaders call white-space opportunities. The opportunities already exist but might require a new configuration of existing skills to harness them. Leaders also need to ask if there is an underserved market—a market currently ignored by others or not well served by others. Think Walmart and the discount store concept for rural Americans or Muhammad Yunus with the microfinance concept for poor women in Bangladesh or Michael Dell with the direct-to-home delivery of computers or Globacom with the introduction of per second billing in mobile telecommunications in Nigeria. They forced the incumbents to change their business strategies as a result. Like French novelist Marcel Proust discovered, "The real voyage of discovery consists not in seeking new landscapes, but in having new eyes."[1] Leaders need to look at their business differently, with new eyes.

Future Opportunities

While looking at your current business will unearth tons of opportunities, most bold dreams will require a peep and a leap of faith into the future. Bold dreams will require some sort of time-travelling into the future to see how the future will be different from the present and to announce that dream to the world. If there is anything we learn from the past it is that the future will be radically different from the present. Only those individuals and firms who can project into the future to see how it will be different from the present and begin the process of creating the future will be winners. The others will either become history or will have to struggle to reinvent themselves to catch up with the winners.

Future opportunities are usually not about incremental improvements of the present. They are usually a break from the present to something radically new and completely different and one that provides a quantum leap in value for customers and the organization. Future opportunities are about possibilities, and possibilities involve a unique point of view about the future even when there is no evidence of the feasibility of it.

The possibilities might be in new market segments (geographical expansion or niche markets), new product offerings, or new customer interfaces. Most of the things we take for granted today were not thought feasible when they were first announced! Great leaders understand how the future might be different from the present and are willing to stake a claim on that future even when the world thinks they are crazy because there are no precedents.

To see the invisible is to do the impossible.

When Steve Jobs launched the first iPhone and Steve Ballmer, former CEO of Microsoft, was asked about the prospect of the phone, he ridiculed it and said,

> Five hundred dollars? Fully subsidized? With a plan? That is the most expensive phone in the world. And it doesn't appeal to business customers because it doesn't have a keyboard, which makes it not a very good email machine.[2]

Today, the rest, as they say, is history. No wonder President Obama said of Steve Jobs when he died, "Steve was among the greatest of American innovators—brave enough to think differently, bold enough to believe he could change the world and talented enough to do it."

This ability to dream a new dream, a bold dream, is a necessary trait of great leaders. They envision a different future today and step out to pursue it even though there are no guarantees of success. Call them the Christopher Columbus of the modern era—they leave the known for the unknown and step out of the boat of comfort and mediocrity to walk on the water to greatness. They are pioneers, trailblazers, and pathfinders. They are not content to follow the beaten path of mediocrity. They sail to the furthest places of the earth to discover unexplored territories.

Three Questions to Unlock Your Creativity about the Future

1. Why are we doing what we are doing? For example:
   a. Why do people go to bookshops to buy books?
   b. Why do we have to wait to see our photographs?
2. Must we continue doing the same things? For example:
   a. Must people go to bookshops to buy books? Will they continue to go to bookshops in the future?
   b. Must we wait before the photographs are printed?
3. How else can we offer the same benefits with a different configuration? For example,
   a. Can you offer the ability to buy books with a different configuration? Amazon.com answered the question.

b. Can you get your photographs immediately? Instant photography and digital photography answered the question.

Current Organizational Resources and Capabilities

Notice that the denominator of our dream equation is current organizational resources and capabilities. Resources are what an organization has, both tangible resources (building, cash, equipment, raw materials, etc.) and intangible resources (brand, patents, etc.). Capabilities are what an organization can do (core competence, knowledge capability, etc.). A lot of African countries, for example, are blessed with an abundance of human and natural resources but are capability impoverished as years of mismanagement of their resources have left most countries in dire conditions. On the other hand, Singapore is a resource-impoverished country with the absence of natural resources but is a capability-rich country because the first prime minister of Singapore, Lee Kuan Yew, invested in developing its national capabilities. Today, Singapore is a powerhouse in Southeast Asia.

The lesson is clear: Without the right leadership, resources will be wasted. To manage resources effectively, leadership must have a vision of what to do with the resources. Depending on resources alone without developing the capabilities necessary for success shows a lack of leadership foresight. Just as nations are handicapped not because of the lack of resources but because of bad leadership, organizations fail not because of the absence of resources but because of their leadership's failure to develop the capabilities needed for success. And it is leadership's vision that determines whether the presence or absence of resources will be a limiting factor for success.

How Big Is Your Dream?

Great leaders know the importance of resources and capabilities for organizational success, but they do not limit their dreams to the size of their current resources and capabilities. In the book, *From Third World to First, The Singapore Story: 1965 – 2000* (HarperCollins Publishers 2000), Lee Kuan Yew narrated how he was able to transform Singapore from a third world country to an economic powerhouse. And at the heart of the transformation is the power of bold dreams. He dreamed of making Singapore one of the world's leading crude oil–refining countries even when the country did not have crude oil deposits. He also dreamed of making Singapore a regional financial hub even though—with a population of just over three million then (now over five million)—it is a small country compared with its neighbors. Had he limited his dreams to the size of the country or the availability of resources, Singapore would not have achieved greatness and become a force to reckon with as it is today. In fact, I believe that if the size of the dream or vision is not greater than the current resources and capabilities by a factor of 10, then that dream is not bold enough.

Here's my guide to measure the size of your dreams:

- *Bold dream:* dream > current resources and capabilities by a factor of 10
- *Good dream:* dream > current resources and capabilities by a factor greater than 1 but less than 10
- *No dream:* dream = current resources and capabilities (more like a plan)
- *Waste:* dream < current resources and capabilities (Waste is the end result of resources and capabilities being greater than one's dreams.)

Great leaders dream big and find ways of acquiring the necessary resources and developing the requisite capabilities to achieve their dreams. It is the size of their dreams that stimulates the accumulation of resources and the development of capabilities and not the other way around. To shrink the size of your dreams to match the resources and capabilities of the organization is to abort the potential of greatness. One test of a bold dream is when the incumbent ignores you because the dream doesn't fit into the existing business models, experts say realizing it is impossible because it has no precedent, and critics condemn you for not being realistic.

Tony Elumelu is a dreamer. He was the first Nigerian CEO to see the future possibilities in other African countries. As the CEO of the then

Standard Trust Bank (now the United Bank for Africa), he pioneered the expansion of Nigerian banks into other African countries. Today, as the chairman of Heirs Holdings, he is pioneering Africapitalism, which is predicated on the belief that Africa's private sector can and must play a leading role in the continent's development.[3] Under his foundation, the Tony Elumelu Foundation, he has set aside $100 million to encourage 10,000 young entrepreneurs across the African continent. That's a bold dream, and I salute his courage. Bill Gates is another entrepreneur with a bold dream—to eradicate malaria from the African continent and the world at large. I salute his courage too.

Courage to Dream

One quality of great leaders is the courage to dream. Why would any sane person dream of something new that would stretch him beyond the current availability of resources? Why dream up something bold when you might be ridiculed or fail? Well, that's the difference between great leaders and mediocre ones. Great leaders are not afraid of failing. Their greatest fear is living life below the realm of their potentials and possibilities. They dream up bold new ventures to push themselves to the limits of their possibilities and to challenge conventional wisdom and common sense to see what is possible. Their curiosity to challenge conventional wisdom redefines the meaning of conventional wisdom.

Progress has never been made within the confines of the known. Those who rewrite history are willing to challenge the wisdom of the day.

Travel by air? Impossible.
Place a man on the moon? Ludicrous.
Wireless communication? Organ transplants? Not a chance.

You get the idea. Had these men and women accepted conventional wisdom, we would still be bound by the limitations of our forefathers. To dream effectively, you must have the courage to challenge the wisdom of your day. So list all the conventional wisdom you know and challenge the wisdom. Bold dreams challenge conventional wisdom to see which should be accepted and which should be discarded. The desire to test reality is perhaps the greatest desire for these leaders.

To see what is possible is often the springboard to do the seemingly impossible!

Make the Dream Meaningful

You have a bold dream? Great, but it will not inspire people until you do something else. You need to inspire hope in your people. Inspiring hope is closely related to dreaming a bold dream, but a little more than it. Dreaming a bold dream is personal. Your bold dream is usually from your perspective—what you hope to accomplish. Inspiring hope is sharing the dream from the perspective of your team and communicating how the dream is important not just to you but also to them and the most important people they care about. *Inspiring hope is speaking to the collective interests of your people.* It is giving voice to the dreams and aspirations of your constituents. It is moving from "I" to "We" in your speech. No matter how fantastic your bold dream is, it won't inspire hope if in communicating the dream, you speak only from your perspective and interests.

Why did Martin Luther King Jr.'s "I Have a Dream" inspire hope and set off a cascade of events that forever changed the history of the American Civil Rights Movement? Simply because it appealed to common interests. He anchored his dream not only on his personal interests but also on the collective interests of people—blacks, Hispanics, and whites. People listened and said to themselves, "I can relate with that. He is giving voice to my concerns and fears. He is speaking to my deepest held values." He talked about the constitution, the Emancipation Proclamation, the Declaration of Independence, and natural laws like justice and equality. He spoke about what they could relate to. In fact, his "I Have a Dream" speech can be revised to "We Have a Dream." Anyone could have given that speech, and nobody would have recognized Martin Luther King Jr. in it. That's the power of speaking to the collective interests of people.

Inspiring hope is sharing your bold dream from the perspective of your people and what they care about. Who would want his children to be judged by the color of their skin and not by the content of their character? He was speaking to them. People could relate to the dream. He gave expressions to their deepest-held values. Don't talk about the vision from your perspective only. Don't also share the vision from the perspective of your organization alone. Share the vision from your constituents' perspectives. People want to be a part of something bigger than themselves. They want to contribute their quota to something that will outlive them, but hate to be used to further someone's personal ambitions.

So start by asking the following questions:

- Why is the dream important to you?
- Why should the dream be important to them—your people? Why should they care about it?

To appreciate the second question, you need to understand that dreams have two components:

- *A future anticipation:* A dream is an event in the future. It is the picture you hold in your imagination of what you would like to do or become.
- *A rewarding adventure:* A dream is also a rewarding adventure. It has rewards attached to it. It not only shows you *what* you want to accomplish or *where* you would like to be in life but also tells you *why* you want to accomplish that goal or become that person. A true dream fulfills hopes and provides great pleasure and satisfaction. Fulfilling your hopes and bringing great pleasure are the answers to the *why* you may have a certain goal. And they are also your rewards. Think about it. Human beings are reward-motivated organisms. The reward determines the pursuit. Like plants that move in the direction of light in order to produce food via photosynthesis, humans are motivated to action when the reward is clear. *Whether the result is intrinsic—a feeling of self-actualization—or extrinsic—in the form of material success—we move only in response to a clear understanding of the reward attached to an action.* This is one reason few people join in the pursuit of others' dreams. They don't know the rewards for embarking on the journey. As a leader, you must define the rewards and communicate them to your team constantly.

Do you want to inspire people? Dream a bold dream and speak of it from "our collective interests" and watch the magnetic effect you dream will have on your team.

My Commitment

"I will not allow the level of available resources or the unavailability of resources to deter me from dreaming big for my organization."

Now go ahead and write specific ways to achieve the commitment you've made.

1. _____
2. _____
3. _____

CHAPTER 8

Grow Your People

My loyalty to you as a follower is a function of the commitment and sacrifice you've made to help me grow.

The best leaders share a common trait: They help their people grow. They do not leave their people how they met them. They help their people to develop new capacities and competencies to perform better on the job. They ensure that their people constantly hone their skills and push the envelope of their talents to deliver extraordinary performance. These leaders can be likened to a refinery. In fact, I call them *people refineries:* They process and purify their people and make them more valuable than they were before they met them. And like crude oil distillation that yields more refined products, their people not only become pure, they become more valuable and productive because they discover new skills and capacities they never knew they had in them.

To join the elite group of leaders, you need to develop the *people refinery* mindset. Leadership comes with responsibilities. Your first responsibility as a leader toward the people under you is to help them develop their skills and capacities to perform better on the job and not to complain about, criticize or condemn them. How do you know that someone is growing? Two ways: An increase in size and also a decrease in dependence. That is, as people grow, they learn to do things by themselves. When people grow, they begin to function, to use their initiative and skills without depending on you.

People come with raw talent and potential, but potential is nothing without the needed push. And it is the specific job of leadership to give potential the needed push—to discover, harness, and deploy it for the benefit of the individual, the organization, and humanity in general. Great leaders look beyond the tons of rubbish of their people to the wealth of potential inside their teams and commit to unearthing it. This process requires faith and patience—faith to believe in the potential of their people and patience to unearth and convert the potential into a finished product, a wonderful masterpiece. And guess what? My loyalty to you as a follower is a function of the commitment and sacrifice you've made to help me grow.

The hallmark of growth is when your people can function effectively, independent of you. Lao Tzu was right when he said,

> To lead people, walk beside them... As for the best leaders, the people do not notice their existence. The next best, the people honor and praise. The next, the people fear; and the next, the people hate... When the best leader's work is done the people say, "We did it ourselves!"[4]

Observe carefully that when the best leader's work is done, the people say, "We did it ourselves!" The goal of great leadership is to pass "the genes of greatness" to the next generation, to reproduce much better clones of oneself. So, ask yourself, what skills have the people you are leading developed under you? What new capacities and competencies have they developed under your leadership? Can they perform better today because of your leadership? What do they know today that they didn't know last year? What can they do today that they couldn't do last year? Are they becoming better or worse under you? When you fail to make them better, they become bitter, and bitter people cannot achieve better results.

So how do great leaders grow their people? I will use the GROW acronym I've developed to explain the process of growth.

G—Gifts (Skills and Competencies)

The starting point of growth is a focus on the skills and competencies of your staff. What skills do they have now (current), and what skills do they need to have (future) to become more effective on the job? I am a corporate trainer and facilitator, and I am grateful to all the organizations that require my services to either train or coach their staff. However, such training and professional coaching needs to be supplemented with the manager's on-the-job coaching, which can never be outsourced.

Great leaders roll up their sleeves and do the "dirty work" of coaching their people. They understand that people are like raw materials: They need to be processed and refined to bring out the best in them. And great leaders do this in four stages as shown in Figure 8.1—what I call "*know, show, observe, cheer.*"

Know

The first stage is that you, the leader, know how to do the job or have developed the requisite skills yourself. You cannot lead people further than you have traveled yourself. Consequently, the first step in developing your people is to commit to your own growth and development. Leadership expert Warren Bennis noted, "It is the capacity of leaders to develop themselves that sets them apart from their followers." How can you give what you don't have? Your followers can only drink from the overflow of your reservoir of knowledge and skills.

Commit to your own growth and development. Under the reign of Julius Caesar, the Roman army was guided by one philosophy: "The soldier has a right to a competent commander." If you transfer this to the workplace, we would say that the staff has a right to a competent manager. You get the idea. Growth begins with you!

Show

The second stage is to teach your people how the job is done. Some leaders do not like to show their people how the job is done; they delight

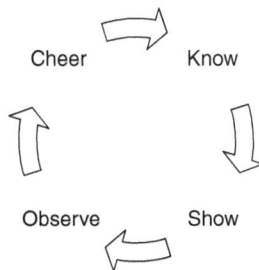

Figure 8.1 Developing your people cycle

in their people making mistakes so that they can shine at their expense. However, great leaders teach their people what they know so that their people will know it too. I told some people recently: "Never follow any leader who will not show you the secrets of his or her success." Take your people through the basics. Teach them the fundamentals. Teach them what you know. Show them how you do it. When they grow, you glow!

Observe

The third stage is to allow your people to do the job while you supervise them. The goal here is to ensure that your people can do it under your guidance. This is more like an apprenticeship scheme. All great professions—medicine, law, engineering, and so on—teach students through an apprenticeship scheme. Institute one yourself. Delegate tasks to your people, so that they can develop their skills through practice, and observe them. As you observe their performance, learn the art of giving immediate feedback to your team.

Cheer

Once you are sure that they have mastered the art and science of the new task, your final role is to inspire them to continuously look for new and better ways of doing the job. Here, your role is that of a cheerleader urging your people on to do a better job.

(Multiply: Although not in the model, this is encouraging the new clone to go and do the same for others, to reproduce himself in his team. By so doing, you are multiplying the growth potential of your team. Each person in your team should have one person under his belt that he is responsible for helping to grow.)

R—Responsibilities

When people grow, they take on new responsibilities without caving under pressure. There is a similarity between a great leader and a great parent. Why do I say so? Because the goal of great parenting is to raise successful, independent children—children who will be independent of their parents but will make decisions that will make their parents proud. It's the same with great leadership—to raise successful, independent leaders. Just as parents increase the authority and responsibilities of their children as they grow through different stages, great leaders do the same with their people. They begin to assign greater responsibilities and decision-making authority to their would-be leaders.

I was privileged recently to address the board of a leading African bank that has decided to increase the responsibility and decision-making authority of its country CEOs. I was thrilled as I know that the organization is on the path of greatness. Great leaders assign greater responsibility with authority to their followers; average leaders, on the other hand, are happy with dependent followers. They take pride in an unhealthy, dependent relationship from their followers, and that's one reason they will remain average at best.

O—Opportunities

Great leaders seek career advancement opportunities for their people. How can people grow if they are not exposed to opportunities? To look for opportunities for your people is to ask how you can help them succeed with their gifts. Here are three simple steps you can take immediately to structure opportunities for the growth of your people. These steps constitute what I call the ATP method.

A—Assignments

People grow when they are given new assignments, like a project to lead, a presentation to make, a proposal to write, and so on. Giving people new and challenging assignments is one way of creating opportunities for growth as your people will be exposed to key influencers in the organization who will notice them. Match the challenge to their gifts or skill, but don't expose them first if you have not shown them how to do the task as it will amount to setting up your people to fail.

T—Transfers

Sometimes great leaders seek opportunities to transfer their staff to a new unit, department, branch, job function, or location just for them to grow. One of the most pathetic examples of not allowing your colleagues

to grow through transfers was an instance mentioned by a training participant some years ago. He had the opportunity to head a Nigerian bank's new
branch in South Africa as the country manager, but his boss vehemently
refused because, according to her, he was her best staff. Without him, her
branch would collapse. The bank had to look for another employee, who
was released by his own manager, and he lost that opportunity. The boss
was only concerned about her own performance and not the growth of
the staff. Great leaders look for ways to expose their people to opportunities that would advance their careers. They would gladly release their best
hands to seek new career opportunities if that would help them grow.

P—Promotions

I cannot overemphasize this point. People cannot grow remaining on the
same level for years. Recommend your people for promotions. Champion
their causes. However, promotions must come with new assignments and
greater responsibilities for them to be meaningful. Promoting someone
to a higher level without increasing his span of responsibilities would
not really further his career. It may make the individuals feel good and
increase their pay but will not help them become better workers in the
long run. Promotion with an increased span of control or with new
responsibilities is the recommended way to help your people grow.

W—Weaknesses

You may be wondering what weaknesses have to do with the model. Is
leadership not about strengths and capacities to perform? Yes, leadership begins with maximizing strengths, but often, leaders are destroyed
by their weaknesses—anger, impatience, greed, unbridled libido, alcohol addiction, drug abuse, and so on. The list of leaders who have been
destroyed by their weaknesses is endless. How many musicians, sports
personalities, and movie actors have died before their time due to alcohol
and drug addictions? How many business leaders have been sacked and
sentenced to prison for fraud and accounting malpractices? Great leaders
help their people grow by helping them overcome their weaknesses—the
challenges that can destroy their futures.

Leadership expert John Maxwell observed, "You can find smart, talented, successful people who are able to go only so far because of the limitations of their leadership." Help your people overcome their weaknesses and watch your leadership effectiveness multiply.

I classify leadership weaknesses into three broad categories:

- *Professional or competency-related weaknesses* are job-related weaknesses, and the *G* aspect of the model will deal with them.
- *Interpersonal weaknesses* are weaknesses related to the staff's ability to work with others—for example, poor listening skills, failure to cooperate effectively with teammates (argumentative and stubborn).
- *Intrapersonal weaknesses* are weaknesses within the individual that have the potential to impede his growth and effectiveness, and they are further divided into three:
  - *Attitudinal challenges* range from the superstar syndrome (Chapter 1) to feelings of insecurity, unworthiness, and lack of self-confidence.
  - *Negative personal lifestyles* include risky and dangerous behaviors that are not allowed by the organization. Most football clubs ban their players from smoking and excessive drinking because of the impact these have on the players' capacity to perform.
  - *Moral challenges* are values-related challenges such as sexual harassment and greed.

Whatever the nature of the challenges, it is the job of a leader to help his people overcome them. The leader is thus a coach, guardian, counselor, and mentor.

You can see how using the GROW model helps both the individual and organization to succeed. Individuals who grow have a healthy dose of high self-esteem and self-efficacy, which leads to increased productivity for the organization. Such individuals will champion the causes of their organizations, remain loyal to their companies (leading to low staff turnover), and take on the role of mentors and coaches for the next generation of leaders.

Organizations win when they replenish their depleting intellectual stock faster than their competition does theirs. And it is the collective replacement that counts. Today's leadership challenges cannot be solved by a solo player no matter how wonderful he is. It is the collective understanding of the team that will solve today's pressing problems. Remember, people are not your most important asset, not even the right people. It is the right people who continually replenish their intellectual stock to continually remain relevant that are your most important asset. Helping your people to grow is the most important strategy of replenishing their depleting intellectual stock.

My Commitment

"I commit to GROWing my team."

Now go ahead and write specific ways to achieve the commitment you've made.

1. _____
2. _____
3. _____

CHAPTER 9

Engage Your Constituents

Engaged employees go over and beyond for the causes of their organizations, leading to a quantum leap in organizational performance.

The 2013 "State of the Global Workplace" report by Gallup paints a very sorry picture of the modern workforce. According to the report, only 13 percent of workers worldwide are engaged or "psychologically committed to their jobs and are likely to be actively contributing to the progress of their organisations."[5]

The bulk of employees worldwide (63 percent), according to the report, are "not engaged"—meaning that they lack motivation and are less likely to invest discretionary effort in organizational goals or outcomes.[6] The rest (24 percent) are "actively disengaged," indicating that they are unhappy and unproductive at work and liable to spread negativity among coworkers.[7]

What a pathetic picture of the current state of the global workforce. This means that most organizations are filled with timekeepers and clock-watchers—people who sit idly watching the ticking of the clock and waiting for their paycheck at the end of the month for just watching the clock! Their hearts and souls are elsewhere. They are both present and absent. They are physically present, but emotionally, they are absent.

These people pose a greater threat to the company's corporate existence than external competition. If the report is anything to go by, only 13 out of 100 persons in your company are interested in your company's success. Is it any wonder that most strategic plans end up in the refuse dump? Think of the effort that you will unleash if you can increase the engagement levels of your staff.

What Is Engagement?

But what exactly is employee engagement? Think of a couple who just got engaged, and you get the idea of what engagement is. I define *engagement* simply as the willingness to say "I do" to the organization and the resultant commitment to follow through with the obligations of "I do."

Engagement is the alignment of the employee's head, heart, and hands with the organization's objectives. It comprises the mutual commitment of the company and the employee at a cognitive level (head) and an emotional level (heart) and the resultant behaviors (hands)—the efforts and sacrifices made to bring to completion something bigger than either the employee or the organization. Engaged employees know what is expected of them (head), are excited about it (heart), and are willing to do over and beyond what is expected (hands).

> Engagement is the alignment between the employee's head, heart, and hands with the organisation's objectives.

Why Engagement?

Engagement results in the capture of discretionary effort, leading to breakthrough results. Engaged employees go above and beyond what is expected of them to deliver business results. Engaged employees put their lives on the line to ensure that their organizations succeed. They subsume their personal interests for the good of their organizations. They care. They care about their organizations, work, customers, and colleagues. What else can you ask for?

But without engagement, people don't care. They only do what is necessary or what they are forced to do. Your bold dream will not inspire them. It will receive a lukewarm response or be dismissed or mocked by disengaged people. Now you understand why engagement matters.

There are several benefits of engagement, but four are particularly important for leaders:

1. *Commitment:* Engagement fosters commitment, leading to increase in productivity. Engaged employees are willing to make the necessary sacrifices to see their organizations succeed because they are committed to their organizations. They see an alignment between their values, goals, and aspirations and those of their organizations. They care about their organizations because they believe that the organization also cares about them. Therefore, they go the extra mile, put in the extra hours, and make the necessary sacrifices for their organizations to succeed.

2. *Positive relationships:* There is a high sense of camaraderie among engaged staff, and this spirit of camaraderie creates a positive atmosphere where people are willing to stand in the gap for one another to ensure that work gets done.

3. *Workplace retention:* Engaged employees are there to stay. They are loyal not because of their paycheck but because they believe in the causes of their organizations and identify with them. They are proud of their organizations and will willingly forego a substantial pay rise to remain in their companies.

4. *Increase in productivity levels:* The end result of engagement is an increase in the productivity levels of the organization. There is a direct correlation between your organization's engagement scores and your bottom-line success.

Levels of Engagement

There are different models and classifications of engagement levels. In my work as a leadership coach and trainer to over thousands of employees in Nigeria and Africa, I can classify employees into five categories based on my experience of employee engagement as shown in Figure 9.1.

Committed

This category marks the highest level of engagement. Using the "I do" concept, these employees are still in love with their initial commitment. Their heads, hearts, and hands are aligned. This group of employees will go over and beyond what needs to be done. They are more likely to take

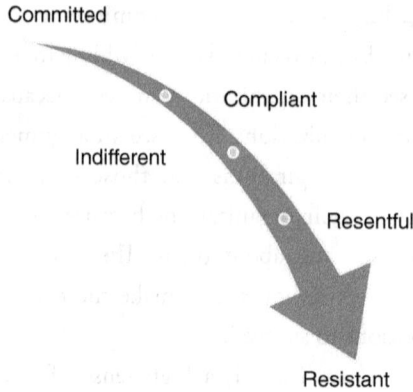

Figure 9.1 Employee engagement levels

initiative and recommend process and product improvements to their organizations. They can be counted upon to deliver excellence.

Compliant

This category of staff has fallen out of love, but they are still hanging in there. Their heads and hands are involved but not their hearts. They may complain, but they will still get the job done. The challenge, however, is that they won't go over and beyond to deliver performance. They won't go the extra mile. They will only do what is necessary and nothing more. They do it because they feel obligated to put in a day's work for a day's pay. Passion, initiative, and sacrifice died a long time ago.

Indifferent

This group doesn't care any longer; the employees have moved on emotionally. Often, they will wait until they are told about what needs to be done before doing it, and even when they do it, they do not care about the quality of their work or output.

Resentful

They are embittered and angry. They feel hurt, betrayed, and used. Some will voice out their resentment; others will not but show lackluster commitment and even wish that the organization fails. They have no stake in the future of the organization and feel that they have wasted a better part of their lives working for an organization that obviously doesn't care about them. Their hands are in their pockets, and they will only bring them out when forced, but their heads and hearts are absent. If you ask them, they will say that their greatest mistake was joining the organization. I know someone who resigned from an organization some years back and said to me, "Maxwell, I feel like a man raped. I wasted the best part of my life working for this organization." His statement typifies the average response of the people in this group.

Resistant

This group of people will not do what needs to be done unless they are compelled to through force, sanctions, or threats. They will sabotage your best efforts if not identified and managed. Their heads, hearts, and hands are not in their work, and sometimes, not even force will make them change their minds.

The Two Chief Culprits of Disengagement

While the Gallup report paints a pathetic picture of the current state of the global workforce, all hope is not lost. You can still fan the flames of passion within your people. People can move from being resistant to being committed with the right strategies in place. But the curious thing about engagement is that it cannot be legislated. You cannot mandate people to become engaged. And there is no one program and no magic medicine that will solve all the disengagement problems in the workplace. Just as you cannot pronounce people man and wife without their consent by way of "I do," you cannot get people committed until they first say "I do" internally to the organization. You can only encourage them to say "I do," but how?

You need to understand that most people who join organizations start out with high engagement scores. So, if 87 percent of the global workforce is currently either disengaged or actively disengaged according to the Gallup report, then the factors that caused their disengagement must reside within their organizations except that you employed the wrong people in the first place. In my view, *the two chief culprits of disengagement are lack of organizational trust and poor working relationships between the employees and the manager as shown in* Figure 9.2. Fix these two, and engagement scores will move northward.

Organizational Trust

People join organizations either because they need a job or they believe in the organization's cause and want to be part of the dream team. For the second group, when they join an organization and discover that the leaders do not walk the talk themselves, they feel disappointed and betrayed and become disengaged. Broken promises, unjust corporate practices, nepotism, and cronyism by organizational leaders are some root causes of disengagement.

The leader and the top management team are usually the first drivers of engagement. Their behaviors and interactions and the policies that they establish create an environment that determines whether people will remain engaged or not. Look no further than the man in the mirror to find out why your people are not engaged. Without organizational trust, people become dispirited. When people are not respected by the organization and its leaders, they withdraw their commitment from the organization and channel it to their own pleasures, and the journey southward from committed to resistant begins. As a leader, begin by accepting full responsibility for the engagement scores of your employees and issue an apology where necessary. No excuses.

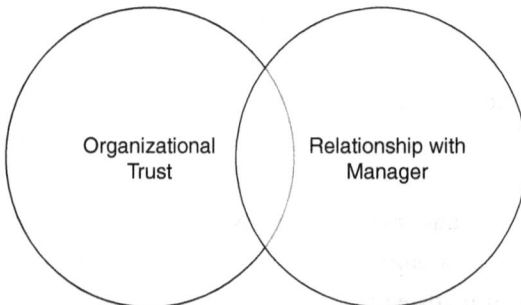

Organizational Trust   Relationship with Manager

Figure 9.2 Increasing employee engagement

Accept responsibility for the organizational mistakes because your bold vision will not inspire wounded and broken souls. What they need is healing, and healing often begins with an apology. You cannot undo the past, but you can begin by acknowledging it, accepting responsibility for it, and making new commitments (not promises) about working on the factors affecting your team. To deny the past and not accept responsibility for it is to abort the future.

Working Relationships between the Manager and Subordinates

Some studies point to the relationship between the manager and the staff as the most important factor in employee engagement. Nothing drives engagement score southward faster than a manager who doesn't exemplify the company's values, uses abusive language to address his team, is seen as weak and incompetent by his staff, doesn't provide enough supervision for his staff, or sets the staff up to fail. Look no further than your managers to find one of the chief culprits when engagement scores are down. Learn to hold your managers accountable for the engagement scores of their workforce. Managers must begin to take responsibility for the way they relate to their people. Their conversations and interactions create the environment that determines whether people will become engaged or not.

Building Engagement

Address the two factors we have identified, and engagement scores will dramatically improve. Other ways to improve engagement scores are as follows:

People-Related Initiatives

Initiatives managers can take to build engagement include the following:

- *Build healthy, collaborative relationships:* Where people see themselves as friends, they are more likely to look forward to going to work. The nature and quality of relationships within your organization are a necessary part of your organizational climate and determine whether people will remain engaged or not. Environments filled with divisions, turf wars, and silo mentality will sap the joy of working and leave people disengaged. Break down the walls of separation. Let people know that we are in this together. Build the bond of togetherness.

- *Treat people with respect:* People cannot become engaged in a disrespectful and abusive environment. Where people feel disrespected, they withdraw their commitment. When managers treat their people like a piece of trash, they begin to despise their managers and their organizations for allowing such managers to thrive in the system. The dominant conservational environment—what people say to one another constantly—must be positive and uplifting if you want your people to become engaged. Negative words weigh down on the heart and kill the human spirit.

- *Offer commensurate rewards:* People who feel used do not become engaged. Reward staff appropriately.

The ability of organisations to reach their next level of greatness is determined by the atmosphere. The atmosphere is determined by the quality of relationships. The quality of the relationships is determined by the quality of the conversations and behaviours.

—Judith E. Glaser, *The DNA of Leadership*

Task-Related Initiatives

The goal of engagement is to get people committed to their work. Task-related initiatives to drive engagement scores upward include the following:

- *Clarifying the big why:* Show people the importance of their jobs and how they connect to the big picture. When people understand the importance of their jobs, it drives their commitment to their work.
- *Enriching job content and providing interesting job assignments:* Routine jobs lead to boredom, and boredom saps the energy and

vitality in people. If you cannot do job rotations, enrich their jobs. Increase their span of control. Provide travel opportunities. Introduce new challenges to spice up the drive to learn something new every day.

- *Providing a clear career path:* When people do not see themselves progressing in their careers, they become disengaged. Why become engaged and go the extra mile when there is no hope of personal growth and progress? Engagement is the mutual commitment of the company and the employee. To demand commitment from your people without making the same commitment to them is at the heart of selfish leaders. Commit to the career development of your staff.
- *Coaching:* Since engagement requires the hands also, building the skills and competencies of your people drives engagement scores upward. When the job at hand matches the skills of the individual (and the reward is appropriate), there is a tendency for him to be engaged, all other things being equal.

Other Organizational Initiatives

- *Providing organizational support—tools and resources:* Empowering people, simplifying processes, and providing work tools often lead to engagement. Where people feel handicapped from achieving their goals due to the lack of organizational resources, they won't go the extra mile.
- *Corporate social responsibility:* People are usually committed to organizations that are not just money-making machines but social enterprises with a heart. Giving staff the opportunity to give back through their favorite charity or social project is another way of increasing employee engagement.

Great things happen when leaders can get their people to say "I do" to their organizations. Like a man who needs to gently woo a woman, leaders need to woo their followers to their causes through tenderness and care, showing their followers why it is in their best interests for them to give their loyalty and heart. Remember, the heart cannot be forced or coerced to love. Force and coercion will drive the heart away, while tenderness will draw the heart toward you. Showing tenderness, building trust, and putting their interests first are the secrets to wooing your employees' hearts. Great leaders ensure that their people's hearts, heads, and hands are aligned to their organization's cause, and it is one secret of extraordinary results.

My Commitment

"I commit to improving the engagement scores of my team."

Now go ahead and write specific ways to achieve the commitment you've made.

1. _____
2. _____
3. _____

CHAPTER 10

Motivate Your Employees

People often say that motivation doesn't last. Well, neither does bathing—that's why we recommend it daily.

—Zig Ziglar

Although leadership is a one-to-many relationship, most leadership interactions occur one-on-one between the leader and individual team members. During such interactions, the leader's goal is to motivate the employee to show greater commitment to his job. While engagement deals with the attitude of the employee toward the company and happens at both the managerial and organizational levels, motivation is more specific. It happens at the managerial level and deals with the employee's attitude toward the task at hand.

Motivating employees is the specific task of leadership. It is the leader's ability to get his people to commit to and follow through with the task before them. And like Zig Ziglar observed, it ought to happen daily. There are some schools of thought that believe you can't motivate people, that you can only inspire them; however, a manager can create an environment—through his words, interactions, and actions—that keeps people motivated.

What Motivates People?

Here are four basic assumptions about motivation that apply to all employees irrespective of their gender, level, education, or race.

People Are Naturally Motivated

When some managers complain that their people are not motivated, they miss a fundamental lesson in motivating people: People are naturally motivated. It's like divinity lit a flame inside every person that keeps burning until death. Motivation is not what you put into people; it is what you bring out of people. It is perhaps for this reason that some say you can't motivate people. They miss the point that the goal of motivating people is not to light a fire in the belly of people but to keep the fire burning and burning for the organization.

People Are Motivated by Different Things and for Different Reasons

Although we are all naturally motivated, we are not motivated by the same things. Some people are motivated by rewards, others by a challenge, yet others by promotions. One of the biggest mistakes leaders make is to use what motivates them as the panacea for all motivational problems. A one-size-fits-all approach doesn't work in motivating people.

People Are Motivated for Their Reasons and Not Ours

Closely related to the previous point is the fact that people are primarily selfish and are only motivated by what is beneficial to them. To motivate your staff, you need to begin by finding out what is meaningful to that individual. People become motivated when something external matches something internal in them—their desires, wants, expectations, and so on. When leaders discover what is meaningful to their people and what drives them, they have in their hands the key to motivating their people.

You Cannot Motivate People Effectively by Executive Fiat

Because motivation is personal, force and decrees cannot motivate people. Force and coercion will give you compliance and even resentment and resistance but not commitment. The problem with force is that the moment you remove the force, the people will slip back into their old mode. You can get people to do almost anything with a gun to their heads, but in the new business era we are in, you cannot motivate people with force.

Motivating Employees

There are several theories of motivation, but eight of the most common are as follows:

Maslow's Hierarchy of Needs

Introduced by Abraham Maslow in 1943, this remains one of the most popular motivational theories. Maslow theorized that human needs are ranked. The most basic level is physiological—food, water, sex, sleep, and so on. The next is safety needs, including economic security, then the needs for love and belonging, esteem, and finally, self-actualization. Applying the hierarchy of needs to the workplace, leaders can do the following:

- *Physiological:* Ensure that the work demands do not affect your employee's health. Too much stress on the job will kill motivation.
- *Safety:* Guarantee a measure of job security and pay people fairly. Reduce occupational hazards.
- *Love and belonging:* Encourage camaraderie, positive relationships among team members, and social bonding.
- *Esteem:* Treat staff with respect. Avoid the use of threatening or abusive words. Make people feel important. Value your staff.
- *Self-actualization:* Create opportunities for growth and provide opportunities for people to fulfill their dreams. Companies like Microsoft, Apple, LinkedIn, and previously, Google allow staff time off to work on their pet projects.

Theory X and Theory Y

In his book *The Human Side of Enterprise*, Douglas McGregor described two opposing ends of dealing with people, what he called Theory X and

Theory Y. Managers using the Theory X approach believe that people are not motivated to work, will resist change, and cannot be trusted with resources. Managers can respond with the hard approach of coercion, micromanagement, or close controls.

Theory Y managers, on the other hand, believe that work can be fun, and given the right resources, people will be committed to doing a good job. The manager's approach will be more of participative management, delegation, and decentralization.

Most managers, from my experience, operate under the assumptions of Theory X, and their management styles reflect their assumptions about people. My take is that managers should begin with a Theory Y mindset and use the Theory X approach when Theory Y has failed. If you have to use more of the Theory X approach, then you either have the wrong people on the bus or there is a problem with your leadership style.

Intrinsic Motivation

This theory simply states that people are naturally more motivated doing some activities than others. Some people find some tasks more fulfilling than others. They enjoy it just for the sake of doing it. For example, I find it more rewarding doing research, developing new concepts, simplifying complex concepts, writing, and teaching compared with doing administrative work, like keeping records.

I remember going for a date many years ago and when I was asked what I did for fun, I replied, "reading." I could see the shock on the lady's face. She said, "I mean 'fun'." And I told her I heard her clearly the first time. I actually derive more fun reading than watching movies or going out. A great leader applying the intrinsic motivation principle will do two things: First, he will find out those activities that his followers consider more rewarding, and second, structure their work to have more of those activities. When people do more of the activities they enjoy, work becomes fun.

Goal-Setting Theory of Motivation

Proposed by Edwin Locke in the 1960s, the essence of this theory is that clear and challenging goals with appropriate feedback are motivating for employees. From this theory came the widely used SMART concept of goal setting. SMART is the acronym that stands for specific, measurable, attainable, realistic, and time specific. Another brainchild of the theory is Management by Objectives, in which the employee and superior jointly set goals or objectives and this is used by the superior to monitor and manage the subordinate's performance. Applying this theory of motivation, managers will set clear, challenging but realistic goals as a means of motivating employees.

Expectancy Theory

This theory was first proposed by Victor Vroom of the Yale School of Management in 1964. It explains why people will choose to exert effort in one activity as against another. He defined *motivation* as "the ability to choose between alternate activities, all controlled by the individual." In his theory, it is the individual who determines motivation, and he does so by the choices he makes internally concerning the task at hand. The expectancy theory states that people will be motivated in putting effort when they believe that their efforts will lead to performance and the reward for achieving the goals is desirable and satisfying.

Vroom introduced three variables within the expectancy theory, which are expectancy (E), instrumentality (I), and valence (V).

- *Expectancy* is the belief that effort will lead to performance or the desired result. Using the expectancy theory, managers who set unrealistic targets will demotivate their staff as the staff will not believe that their efforts will tilt the performance scale. Expectancy says people must feel that they can achieve the desired results to be motivated. Therefore, managers must build people's confidence to motivate them and break the targets into small, workable steps to keep them motivated.
- *Instrumentality* is the belief that once the desired result is achieved, the staff will receive the promised reward. Under this concept, organizations must ensure that promises made to motivate staff to achieve the goals are honored. Once trust is broken or employees feel that the organization will not reward them for meeting their targets, they will not be motivated.

- *Valence* is the value attached to the reward. The rewards must be tied to what the employee values and must be commensurate with the effort required to achieve the results. For example, what is the value of a cheap pen that the employee can buy?

Equity Theory

Developed by Stacy Adams in 1963, this theory postulates that people seek equity between the inputs they bring to a job and the outcomes that they receive compared with the inputs and outcomes of others. While valence of the expectancy theory asks if the employee values the reward, the equity theory asks whether the reward is fair compared with that of others. On the basis of the equity theory we can say that preferential treatment not based on transparency and meritocracy will demotivate people. To keep people motivated using the equity theory, leaders must ensure that people are treated in an equitable and transparent manner.

Positive and Negative Reinforcement

This approach involves the use of external rewards and punishment to change behaviors and encourage motivation.

However, care must be taken with the use of rewards and sanctions. Excessive use of rewards will kill intrinsic motivation and might not be valued after the initial stages (expectancy theory) and puts you at a risk of going against the equity theory, especially when the rewards are discontinued. Rather than becoming a motivational tool, they become an entitlement. Excessive use of sanctions, on the other hand, will make you a Theory X manager. You get the idea. Use external rewards and sanctions sparingly, only when absolutely necessary.

Empowerment

This theory posits that giving people more autonomy in their jobs increases motivation. Empowerment must come with boundaries and accountability for it to be effective.

There are other motivational theories not covered here but these eight captures the essence of most motivational theories.

Applying The Eight Theories of Motivation

- *Maslow's hierarchy of needs:* Understand where people are and align motivation accordingly. At lower levels, financial rewards matter. At middle levels, relationships count. And at higher levels, achievement and advancement are the keys. As a leader, you should combine all three.
- *Theories X and Y:* Believe that people want to do a good job, and relate to them accordingly.
- *Intrinsic motivation:* Structure work to ensure that people do daily what they find most rewarding.
- *Goal-setting theory:* Set SMART goals for employees and provide appropriate feedback to them.
- *Expectancy theory:* Ensure that goals set are realistic, and the rewards are personalized and meaningful. Honor your promises once goals are met.
- *Equity theory:* Treat people fairly and in a transparent manner.
- *Positive and Negative Reinforcement:* Use rewards and sanctions as appropriate. Note the aforementioned caution.
- *Empowerment:* Give people autonomy within boundaries and hold them accountable for results.

A Simple Motivational Chart

Remembering the eight theories is not easy, and I understand, so I have distilled the theories into a simple motivational chart (Figure 10.1) that combines some or all of them.

Needs (Maslow's theory): What are your people's needs, and how can you tie the results you desire to one of their needs? For example, if the person is at the esteem level, can you sell the task from the perspective of the respect and recognition he will get from completing the task?

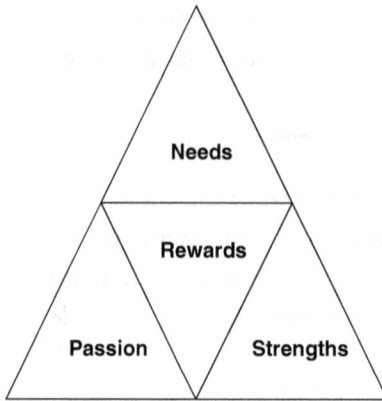

Figure 10.1 **A simple motivational chart**

Passions (intrinsic motivation): Does the activity align with his passions? If it doesn't, can you sell it from the perspective that it is an enjoyable activity and enjoin him to give it a try?

Strengths (goal-setting theory, expectancy theory): Can he do it? How confident is he to take on the task?

Rewards (expectancy, equity, positive reinforcement): What are the rewards? Are they fair? Will they be valued?

Motivating Employees—The Final Piece

All the theories of motivation and my simple motivational chart are useless if this piece is not in place. Actually, this piece is the foundation of motivation, without which the eight theories will not work. What is this piece? *Motivation begins with you, the leader!* If you are not motivated yourself, people will pick up the cues from you and act accordingly. A leader who is not motivated is like an environment without air—suffocating—and will quench the fire in his people.

To motivate others, you need to be motivated yourself. It is the principle of authenticity. Your words, actions, and behaviors must convey to your people that you are motivated and want to achieve results, and even without understanding any of the aforementioned theories, over

50 percent of your work is done if you are genuinely motivated. So just before you blame your people for not being motivated, take a look at the person in the mirror and ask, Am I really motivated myself? Remember, *the greatest motivational principle in the universe is the power of a positive example!*

My Commitment

"I commit to motivating my employees through the power of a positive example and by applying the relevant motivational theories."

Now go ahead and write specific ways to achieve the commitment you've made.

1. _____
2. _____
3. _____

CHAPTER 11

Unify Constituents around a Common Cause

The final test of a leader is that he leaves behind him in other men, the conviction and the will to carry on.

—Walter Lippmann

The Arab Spring, which led to changes in governments in Tunisia, Egypt, and Libya and policy modifications in Yemen, Bahrain, Morocco, and other Arab countries, started with one man: Mohamed Bouazizi. According to reports, on December 17, 2010, his wares were confiscated on the streets of Tunis, and he was harassed and publicly embarrassed. Unable to withstand this, he set himself on fire in front of a local municipal office. That act of self-immolation led to widespread protests, called the "Jasmine Revolution", beginning on December 18, 2010, in Tunisia, and forced President Zine el-Abidine Ben Ali to resign on January 14, 2011, after 23 years in power. Although we can say that the Arab Spring started with Bouazizi, he alone could not have caused the widespread changes that happened as a result.

Usually, leadership begins with one person or a few people—from Rosa Parks's refusal to give up her seat to John F. Kennedy's "man in the moon" speech to Mohamed Bouazizi's act of self-immolation. However, results are impossible without the adoption, personalization, and pursuit of the vision by key strategic people. Some call it teamwork, others call it building coalitions and strategic alliances, and yet others call it stakeholder management. But I prefer the phrase *creating a movement*.

Without understanding the power of movements, the ignorant and uninitiated will celebrate the heroic acts of single individuals, not realizing that nothing great has ever been conceived and built by a single individual without the contributions of others. The talk of being self-made is a fallacy. Nobody ever accomplished greatness without the support of others in their lives. Self-driven, yes. Self-made, absolutely no!

Leadership begins with you, yes. But leadership cannot be achieved without others. Even our working definition of leadership as relationships × results negates the theory of one-man leadership. As a leader, you must unify people with disparate interests into a harmonious group and create a movement to achieve your goals. You must get them to give up their personal interests for the group's interests. You must get them to look out not only for themselves but also for others. Failure to do so guarantees that results will be illusory. Without movements, visions die unaccomplished, expectations go unfulfilled, and obstacles remain unmovable. But with movements, almost nothing is impossible.

What is a movement? The best way to define a *movement* is by comparing it to a tsunami. A movement is not just a group of people working together to achieve a common goal (that's teamwork); it also includes their willingness to stake their very existence and lives for the accomplishment of that purpose. The people who protested in the Arab Spring staked their lives and existence for that cause. And truly, nothing can stop a group of people who are willing to stake their very existence for the accomplishment of a set goal.

Movements happen when people adopt the cause, personalize it, pursue it, and are willing to sacrifice their lives for it. Please note that sacrificing one's life here does not mean dying but the willingness to go the extra mile, ploughing all of one's resources into one's cause, burning the midnight candle to achieve results, or just plain hard work.

Movements and Teamwork

Since movements begin with teamwork, let's briefly talk about the latter. Here are some elements that guarantee high-performance teams:

The Vision, Goal, and Objective of the Team Must Be Clear and Inspiring

Movements start with a vision; however, when the vision is not clear and unifying, divisions, cliques, and turf protection are the end results. An inspiring vision appeals to the collective interests of everybody in the team. People who rioted in Tunisia did not do so just because of Mohamed Bouazizi; they rioted for themselves—to prevent what happened to Bouazizi from happening to them. People will not sacrifice their lives unless it appeals to their collective interests.

Teams Must Be Committed to the Same Organizational Objective

In teams, there is only one purpose, one aim, and one objective—the organization's purpose. In an effective team, people have subordinated their personal interests for the good of the team. Commitment to the same purpose is the willingness to sacrifice personal interests for the good of the team. Teams fail where members cannot subordinate their personal interests for the good of the team.

Each Member's Complementary Skills Must Be Utilized to the Fullest

Peter F. Drucker writing in *Management: Tasks, Responsibilities, Practices* says,

> It is the test of an organization to make ordinary human beings perform better than they seem capable of, to bring out whatever strength there is in its members, and to use each man's strength to help all the other members perform. It is the task of organization at the same time to neutralize the individual weaknesses of its members.

Teams are a microcosm of the larger organization, and they should help individuals contribute their best by focusing on complementary skills. With the focus on complementary skills within the team, team members become intrinsically motivated and fired up for success as everyone's skills are appreciated and valued.

Each Member Must Contribute Effectively to the Team

While complementary skills point to the different types of skills each member brings to the team, contribution is the value they add. A team will not function effectively if team members are deadweights on the team. Teamwork is not a guise to shield poor performers. It is called *teamwork* for a reason. Each member of the *team* must *work* and show their contributions to the team. And team members must hold one another accountable for performance.

Open Communication

Communicating upward, downward, and across the team is vital (see chapter 15 on communication). Motivation goes out of the window if team members cannot share their concerns about some personal or work-related issue. You must also avoid the situation where some people in the team try to dominate discussions and want to always be heard. Everyone must be given equal opportunity to speak and be heard. When people feel that their opinions don't count, they conclude that their contributions aren't necessary. That is, opinions and contributions go together. Where I feel my opinions are respected, I will do everything in my power to give my best and vice versa.

Incentives and Consequences

This is the use of rewards and sanctions to encourage positive behaviors and discourage negative behaviors, respectively. Team members who fail to align with the purpose, vision, or goal of the team even after counseling and coaching have taken place should be removed. To keep a poor performer on a team is one sure way to discourage high performers.

Strong and Appropriate Leadership Styles

Without strong and courageous leadership, the team will wither in the pursuit of its goal. The type of leadership that works best in teams is situational and rotational, one that allows different people to take the lead, on the basis of whose competence and skills best suit the task at hand.

Team Composition

Perhaps nothing is more important in teamwork than the issue of team composition. Getting the wrong people on board is a recipe for disaster no matter the motivational talks and team-building activities you conduct for them. Team composition simply answers these questions: Who should be in the team on the basis of the work output expected (team makeup)? And how should they relate to one another (team charter)?

Team Makeup

To constitute your team, you need to begin by asking yourself some important questions:

- What are the key deliverables?
- What is the nature of the tasks and subtasks?
- What kinds of skills are required to complete the tasks?
- What is the minimum number of people required for maximum effectiveness?
- What personal characteristics of the individuals are important?

Without answering these questions, teamwork is dead on arrival.

Team Charter

Your team charter is the modus operandi of your team, that is, the team contract. It contains your team norms, the behaviors that would be tolerated and punished by the team. It answers the following questions:

- What will the team ground rules be (e.g., where and when to meet, attendance expectations, workload expectations)?
- How will decisions be made (e.g., consensus, majority vote, leader rules)?
- What potential conflicts could arise in the team and how would they be resolved?

Nothing else determines the productivity of teams like team norms. The problem I have seen in most teams is that there are no norms; they operate an ad hoc model of leadership. There is no proper foundation-laying ceremony as it were where the expectations are communicated to all.

A sample team charter that my teammates and I designed at the London Business School Sloan Masters program in 2010 is given next as a guide. It was signed by the five of us in the team.

Goals

- To create a learning environment in which team members can learn from one another and from each assignment
- To strive to produce output that each team member can take pride in and to receive positive feedback from the class and faculty for the quality of our work
- To have fun and maintain harmony in team meetings and among team members
- To maintain practical focus in our work

Attendance and Participation Expectations

- Attendance at meetings and meaningful contributions are expected and mandatory for all team members.
- A quorum of four team members is required for meeting to go ahead.
- Members are expected to notify the team beforehand in case of absence from or lateness to team meetings.
- Each member is responsible for completing all prerequisite assignments before meetings.
- No personal arguments or criticisms during team discussions.
- Late night or weekend meetings should be avoided where possible.
- Each team member is to organize one social event fortnightly.

Team Roles

- Organizing team meetings is to be rotated among team members fortnightly.

- Each organizer is to arrange feedback of the team activities at the end of his or her period.
- Leading team meetings and presenting work assignments are to be rotated among team members.
- Workload among team members is to be shared equally.

Decision Rules

- Team decisions will be based on qualified consensus principle.
- Any member of the team can call for a time out if or when team meetings degenerate into intense argument between two team members.

Rule Violations and Conflicts

- Rule violations are to be discussed every fortnight.

This team charter "saved" us many times. If we didn't have the rule that states that when discussions become heated, a team member can call for time out, we may have come to blows. Sometimes discussions become so heated and one of us will say "time out" and that's it. By the time we are back, our emotional intensity has been lowered and we can reengage more objectively and constructively.

From Teams to Movements

Movements, like I noted earlier, begin with teamwork but go one step further to include team members' willingness to stake their very existence for the accomplishment of the team's purpose. The additions to the characteristics of teamwork are *a culture of discipline* and *the spirit of sacrifice*. We have already talked about sacrifice earlier so our focus here will be on the culture of discipline.

A culture of discipline is one in which excuses are not tolerated; team members show up irrespective of how they feel and carry out their tasks. It is a culture that is characterized by three things:

Strong Determination to Achieve One's Aim

Movements are like a tsunami because of their ferocious resolve and single-minded focus, however unlike a tsunami, they are constructive in nature. In movements, there is a fanatical focus on business results. Nothing else matters. Everything is judged from one perspective—results.

Low Tolerance Threshold for Mediocrity

In movements, mediocrity is not tolerated, whether from family or friends. They know what is at stake. You either shape up or are shipped out. Your right to remain as an employee is contingent upon your performance. It is a high-performance culture, one that is positively and transparently ruthless in its performance orientation. Think General Electric under Jack Welch.

No Time for Petty Quarrels

People who are struggling to dominate their market do not have time for the arrangement of flowers in the garden. *When people lose sight of their overarching goal, they focus on themselves, which is the root cause of all quarrels—the preservation of one's interests with a bloated sense of self.* In movements, because people are so consumed with breaking world records, beating the competition, and securing the next big patent, for example, they do not have time for petty quarrels.

My Commitment

"I commit to building an effective team and creating a movement from the team."

Now go ahead and write specific ways to achieve the commitment you've made.

1. _____
2. _____
3. _____

SECTION 3

Achieve Extraordinary Results

We have come a long way in our exploration of leadership and what great leaders do. If I may summarize in a sentence what great leaders do, I'd say that they *create value,* as a leader is known by the *unique value* he creates. This is the key difference between real leaders and sit-tight positional leaders. Leaders create value for their constituents, value that would not have been created without their leadership. They look for opportunities to add value to their organizations and their people. Therefore, to measure a leader's effectiveness, look for the unique value that he is creating for his people and the organization he serves and not in the position he occupies or how long he has been in that position.

Our definition of leadership is relationships $\times$ results, and results are seen in value creation, whether strategic, operational, or tactical value. If you are not creating value, measurable value, you are not leading! Leadership is a journey and embarking on a journey means progress toward a destination. So if you are not making progress, then you are not leading. And progress is measured by your organization (organizational viability, bottom line result), shareholders (shareholder value), employees (employee retention, talent management and every other thing under the concept called employee value proposition) and customers (customer value proposition). The value a leader creates must be judged through these four filters.

Here is a chart that we can use to classify leaders on the basis of value creation:

Type of leader	Organizational situation
Ineffective	*Struggling* Destruction of value—the organization is worse off. Negative absolute or relative growth rate Growth rate slower than major competitors
No difference	*Survivor* No net value creation; any growth is due to business effects.
Marginally effective	*Success* Growing marginally faster than competitors Gradually becoming a major force in the industry
Transformational	*Significance* Growing much faster than competitors Redefining industry standards with new innovative products and services

In this section, we will focus on the specific things that a leader has to do to create extraordinary results in addition to everything we have covered.

This section will cover the following nine topics:

- Wonders happen in an atmosphere of positive stretch and fair rewards
- Trust improves the bottom line
- The six essentials every leader must communicate
- Open the channels of communication upward, downward, and across
- Focus on excellence in execution
- Hold your people accountable for results
- Question-based leadership
- Judge performance accurately
- X-ray successes and failures and institutionalize lessons

CHAPTER 12

Wonders Happen in an Atmosphere of Positive Stretch and Fair Rewards

A leader takes people where they want to go; a great leader takes people where they don't necessarily want to go but ought to be.

—Rosalynn Carter

Want to achieve extraordinary results? Then create an atmosphere of positive stretch and fairs rewards.

In today's highly competitive and globalized world, leaders are judged by the results they produce. While the abilities to set direction, mobilize individual commitment, and create a motivating climate for the workforce are noble leadership qualities, in the absence of results, constituents might not be patient enough to give the leader another opportunity to lead them. In politics, leaders have years to prove their worth; in sports like football, usually a year or two, and sometimes just months. Today's business environment is unforgiving without results.

To achieve results, great leaders add another secret ingredient to spice up their leadership effectiveness in addition to everything else that has been written in the previous chapters: They positively stretch their people and compensate them handsomely. Rosalynn Carter was apt in her observation that a great leader takes people where they don't necessarily want to go but ought to be. If you observe carefully, a great leader is different from an ordinary leader in one regard: She has the desire to ensure that her people get to where they ought to be or become what they are capable of becoming even if it means pushing them beyond what they thought was possible.

An ordinary leader is content to allow people to produce at their pace. Not so for a great leader. These leaders inspire, yes, but sometimes even push their people to produce extraordinary results. The truth is that most people do not know what they are capable of producing until they are pushed. The leader's push becomes the elixir that transforms ordinary followers to world changers and history makers. The leader's push helps the followers discover their wings of greatness like the mother eagle's push that helps the eaglets discover that they already possess the capacity to fly.

To positively stretch their people, leaders must understand two essentials—the capabilities of their people and their current performance. Capabilities deal with what they can produce, more like future possibilities not yet realized. Current performance is what they are producing. For many people, their current performance falls short of their capabilities or potential, what I call the potential–performance gap. This gap reflects the absence of leadership. Anytime you see a chasm between potential and performance, you know that leadership is missing as the goal of leadership is to bridge the gap between potential and performance, to ensure that people become everything they are capable of becoming. Leaders, as it were, are bridge builders, building bridges between their constituents' potential and performance.

Great leaders are not satisfied with just performance. They are only satisfied when their people give their best and their all to achieve breakthrough results. Nothing but the best is good enough for them. They are demanding. They are stubborn. They are sometimes ruthless. They can be difficult when it comes to people giving less than their best. But they are not wicked. They do it with the staff's interests at heart. They know what their people are capable of and are willing to shove and push, and they put pressure until their people achieve everything they are capable of achieving or the gasoline tank of potential becomes empty. . The question for this group of leaders is not what their people have achieved but what they achieved compared with what they could have achieved if they had given life their best. John Wooden, the Hall of Famer American collegiate basketball coach, exemplifies this attitude. He won seven NCAA titles in a row and nine titles in 10 years. Three titles in a row is unheard of as no other collegiate basketball coach has won more than two consecutive titles, not to mention seven titles in a row. How was he able to do that? Simply by getting his players to keep improving daily. He pushed them beyond their reach but within their capabilities, beyond what they thought was possible but what he knew was possible. One of his personal philosophies is, "Success is peace of mind that comes from knowing that you gave life your best to become the best you are capable of becoming." I like the idea of the peace of mind that "comes from knowing that you gave life your best."

Can you be a bit honest with yourself? If you had given life your best efforts from the outset, would you be where you are right now? If everyone in your organization is giving their best every day, would your organization be where it is right now? I am sure that the answer would be "No." So even though we have achieved some measure of success in the past, what we have achieved is minuscule compared with what we could have achieved if we had given life our best and lived life on the edge of our potential. Perhaps the missing ingredient is not potential or capacity as we already have the capacity to achieve great things. The missing ingredient is leadership—leadership that challenges us to go out on a limb, to leave the boat of mediocrity, and to become all that we can become. Ralph Waldo Emerson rightly noted that "our chief want in life is someone who will inspire us to be what we know we could be." Breakthrough results happen when leaders inspire their people to push beyond their self-imposed limitations—beyond their current performance but within their capabilities.

How Do Leaders Positively Stretch Their People?

Figure 12.1 shows four categories of employees in organizations using what I call the capabilities–performance targets matrix.

Figure 12.1 The capabilities–performance targets matrix

There are two kinds of *average* people in organizations—average because of limitations in their capabilities and average due to motivation challenges. The first group of people are already performing at their best and cannot perform any more than they are currently performing; the second group can do more but are not motivated to do so. No amount of motivational mantra will make the first group high performers. Positive thinking cannot turn a hen into an eagle or a lizard into a crocodile or a cat into a cheetah. And this realization is liberating for the leader.

No matter how high performing an organization is, there will always be some people who are average; the challenge is to ensure that they are not more than 10 to 20 percent of the workforce. One way of differentiating the capability-limited average people from the motivationally challenged average people is simply this: Motivation and engagement will not affect the first group but will improve the performance of the second group. So, the next time you have an average performer, ask yourself whether this is a result of capability or motivation before you design your strategy to help.

Boredom results when the current job is not challenging enough for the staff—that is, they are currently underutilized. In finance, the term used to find out the utilization of assets is *return on asset*, or the *asset utilization capacity*. For this group of staff, their potential–capability utilization ratio is low. They are far more capable than what they are currently producing, and their current production level might be due to the fact that they are caught in a mundane job or are not trusted with more responsibilities.

Discouragement, on the other hand, occurs when the expectations are way too high for the staff to meet. The expectancy theory of motivation kicks in when the targets are unrealistic.

The New Smart Way of Achieving Results

High performance happens when the job is challenging enough to bring out the best in the employee who has the capacity and motivation to achieve it. And this happens through positive stretch and fair rewards. But how do leaders positively stretch their people? They break down their bold vision into concrete goals and objectives using the well-known SMART acronym but with a little distinction.

- They not only make the goal specific, they also make it *stimulating* and exciting. A specific goal is concrete; a stimulating goal is one that pumps adrenaline into the bloodstream of employees. With a specific goal, people know what they are supposed to do; with a stimulating goal, they cannot wait to get started.

- They not only make the goal measurable, they also make it *meaningful.* They communicate the goal not only from the organization's perspective but also from the individual's perspective. With a measurable goal, people know what you will inspect; with a meaningful goal, they know why they need to achieve the result.

- They not only make sure the goal is attainable, they also make it *action oriented.* They define the key behaviors that the employee must adopt to ensure that the goals are met. There are no ambiguities, no second-guessing, no "Where do we go from here?" look on the faces of their staff. With an attainable goal, they know they can achieve it; with an action-oriented goal, they know what they need to do to achieve it.

- They not only make sure that the goal is realistic, they also make it *rewarding.* They don't make it easy for their people to achieve their goals. They make it rewarding. Making it rewarding will happen when people must stretch, to reach within themselves and harness their talents, skills, resources, and emotional energy to achieve outstanding results. And guess what? The greatest rewards people get for stretching themselves is the self-realization of previously self-imposed limitations. The epiphany that they are far more capable than they thought was possible cannot be quantified in monetary terms.

- They not only make the goal time bound, they also make it *time sensitive.* They create a sense of urgency about the goal.

Providing *stimulating, meaningful, action oriented, rewarding,* and *time sensitive goals* is the new SMART way of thinking for leaders. These are the five ingredients that breakthrough leaders add to goal-setting to stretch their people and achieve outstanding results.

Fair Rewards

Great leaders adequately compensate their people. Rewards are both tangible and intangible, intrinsic and extrinsic. Broadly, the rewards people get for achieving extraordinary results can be classified into three:

- The self-satisfaction that they derive from what they have achieved
- The tangible rewards that they get for their achievements
- The self-realization of who they have now become in the process

And guess what? The greatest of the three rewards is the self-realization of who they have now become (the changes that have taken place in them during their pursuit). Positive stretch changes people in the process of achieving results just as giving birth fundamentally changes a woman's makeup and psyche beyond just giving birth. Beyond the success of realizing their dreams and the rewards associated with such successes, they found the journey far more rewarding and the transformation far more exhilarating than just the accumulation of wealth or personal awards. The persons they have now become far outweigh the successes they achieved. Some develop new and amazing skills; others develop self-confidence and self-mastery; yet others temperance and compassion. Some have scars to show for their journeys; others transcended their initial dreams and goals, going from one innovation and success story to another. But despite the differences in their success stories and journeys, there is a common denominator, a common thread in their tapestry of greatness: Their greatest victory was internal—winning the battle against fear, anxiety, uncertainty, and worries. For example, when people go on a weight loss program and lose weight, we see the three factors working in concert. First, they are happy that they have achieved their goal. The second benefit is the tangible reward of being able to wear the kind of dresses they want. But the most important reward is the self-confidence that it gives them that they can control their own lives and destinies. The third reward is the fuel that drives them on to make major changes in the other areas of their lives. It becomes the secret sauce of their greatness, the elixir that causes them to take on their fears. They take on other projects because of the self-belief that if they can make a change in one area of their lives, they can make changes in other areas as well. It is like David taking on Goliath. He remembered that he had killed the lion and the bear. That self-confidence propelled him to take on Goliath and redefined the competitive landscape. Apple Inc.'s successes with the iPod and iTunes fueled its corporate belief that it will succeed with the iPhone and iPad even against market wisdom. As an organization, the previous successes have changed the company's DNA as it were. That's one reason John Wooden won seven titles in a row. He focused on changing the people in the process.

Changed people achieve extraordinary results because the discipline, sacrifice, confidence, passion, and other qualities required to achieve greatness are now wired into their DNA such that they have no choice but to achieve greatness. Even if they decided not to, it's almost impossible for them. The person they have now become cannot tolerate anything less than excellence. Little wonder Aristotle said, "We are what we repeatedly do. Excellence, therefore, is not an act but a habit." Excellence has become the new normal for them. They cannot help but give their best even if they are not well paid!

My Commitment

"I commit to creating an environment of positive stretch and fair rewards for my team."

Now go ahead and write specific ways to achieve the commitment you've made.

1. _____
2. _____
3. _____

CHAPTER 13

Trust Improves the Bottom Line

High-trust environments create organizational vitality that causes people to go over and beyond what is required of them to achieve outstanding results.

Want to achieve extraordinary results? Then build a high-trust culture!

The admission by Volkswagen in September 2015 that it installed a secret "defeat device" software in the engines of its cars to manipulate fuel emissions during testing was shocking and scandalous. This revelation led to a 30 percent fall in its share price, the resignation of the CEO with more heads set to roll, and punitive fines estimated at about $14 billion.[1]

The question people asked at that time was, "Can Volkswagen regain customers' trust?" The newly appointed chief executive, Matthias Mueller, said his most urgent task was to win back customers' trust. If his most urgent task was to win back customers' trust, then it means that the most important task for any CEO or any company is to retain the trust of the company's customers, business partners, and employees. We don't have to wait for a monumental scandal to realize that without trust, nothing else matters. All our successes can evaporate in a minute in the absence of trust. Ask Lance Armstrong, Marion Jones, or Ben Johnson. Or ask Volkswagen. If the cost of breaching trust would be worth up to $14 billion, then it means that trust is worth at least that much to Volkswagen.

Trust, the issue nobody likes to discuss but one that determines the long-term survival of relationships, is a critical component of leadership. Trust is the glue that binds followers to their leaders, customers to organizations, and supporters to their clubs. Without trust, relationships will disintegrate, customers will leave in droves, and investors will dump the company's shares. On a personal level, will you follow someone you cannot trust or someone you are not sure will keep and honor his word? In like manner, no customer likes to transact a business relationship with an organization with issues of trust.

Trust Defined

There are several definitions of trust, but here are my two personal favorites:

Integrity of People, Systems, and Processes

Trust occurs when the three most important organizational components—people, systems, and processes—have what I call *institutional integrity.* Integrity of people is revealed in their behaviors—no unethical behaviors. Integrity of systems and processes is revealed in the organization's ability to deliver what was promised in advertisements. One way to answer the integrity question is to ask,

- Do our people embody our corporate values in their relationships with one another and customers consistently across our different departments and branches?
- Do our systems and processes consistently deliver on our promise to our customers?

If you cannot answer "Yes" to both, then trust is missing in your organization.

Ease of Doing Business with

My second definition of trust is the *ease of doing business with,* which is the end result of integrity of systems and processes. How easy is it for the organization to deliver on its brand promise? How easy and convenient is it for customers to do business with the organization? Most organizations operate with a mindset of low trust, and this leads to excessive controls and multilayer approval processes. Are some controls necessary? Definitely! However, multilayer approvals are often a reflection of the absence of trust and make it difficult for customers to do business with the organization. Such organizations are *control centric,* not *customer centric.*

The two components of trust can be seen from the internal dimension (the people perspective) and the external dimension (the ability to consistently deliver on our brand promise to customers).

Internal Dimension: Absence of Trust

Here are some symptoms of the absence of trust within an organization:

- Team members are suspicious of one another. Advice and constructive feedback are withheld.
- Team members are not happy to be part of the team. They avoid teammates and team meetings where possible.
- Cliques abound ("us versus them" syndrome, internal divisions, set-up-to-fail syndrome, internal politicking).
- People are interested in preserving their personal agendas rather than promoting the goals of the team; they undermine the team's goals behind the team (backstabbing).
- People say little or nothing during team meetings or communicate only good news; they avoid bad news by all means even if the boat is sinking.
- There is a silent war between management and staff.
- There are multilayer approval processes leading to delay in getting approvals and slow turnaround time in meeting customer needs.
- The environment is very punitive (high-handed and ham-fisted leadership approach and interactions).
- Staff welfare and remuneration packages are poor, coupled with the lavish lifestyles of the leaders.
- Conflict in low trust cultures takes two extremes:
  - *Kill the messenger:* Shoot down every suggestion even when the suggestion is great for the team (finding faults).
  - *Artificial harmony:* Say nothing even when the idea or decision is wrong.

External Dimension: Absence of Trust

Some of the manifestations are as follows:

- Promises are made to entice customers with no intention of delivering on those services.
- Products are packaged to deliver what the organization knows it cannot deliver.
- Accounts are forged to make the company look good or understated to avoid payment of taxes.
- Customers are exploited through hidden charges and exorbitant fees.
- Customers pay for services they don't get.

Building (Rebuilding) Trust

So how do you build trust? In Figure 13.1, I provide my acronym for trust:

T—Truthfulness: In high-trust environments, truthfulness and honesty are valued. People speak honestly about the issues affecting them and confront one another with the facts and do not hide

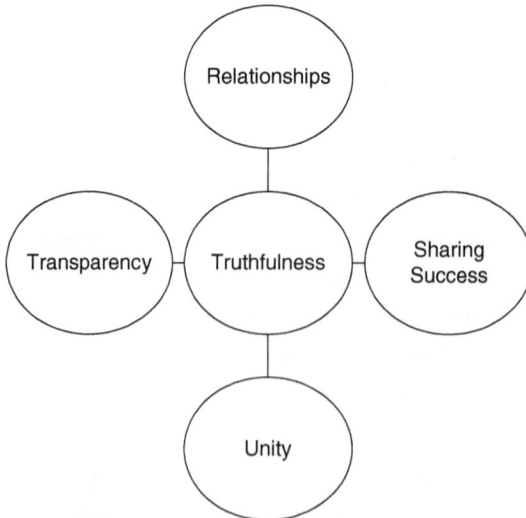

Figure 13.1 The TRUST acronym or framework

the truth. Where truthfulness is practiced, difficult conversations are held, and people hold one another accountable.

R—*Relationships:* In high-trust environments, people feel "We are in this together." People value one another and go the extra mile for one another.

U—*Unity:* Divisions and cliques are reduced to minimum in high-trust environments. Such cultures have a high sense of camaraderie.

S—*Sharing success:* Because we are in this together, rewards are shared. There cannot be trust where some are rewarded for the performance of the team and others are not.

T—*Transparency:* High-trust environments are transparent environments—they walk their talk.

By using the TRUST acronym and applying it to the external and internal dimensions, trust can be built or rebuilt from the two dimensions.

Internal

- *Be truthful with your team:* Nothing kills trust faster than telling outright lies or coloring the truth. Say it as it is. Let people know what they need to know. Truthfulness is the first ingredient of trust. Don't make promises you have no intention of keeping.

- *Create an environment where people know what is happening and can ask for clarification:* When people don't know what's happening in the organization, they second-guess your intentions, often jumping to the wrong conclusions, which makes trust impossible. Don't allow people to second-guess your actions. Communicate always.

- *Build healthy, collaborative relationships:* Trust is the glue that binds relationships together. When people have healthy relationships, they trust one another. Nip interpersonal problems in the bud. Value people. Make people feel important. Create the bonds of togetherness. Break down the walls of separation.

- *Share rewards with the team:* There cannot be trust when rewards are shared at the top and the foot soldiers only hear about them. The fact that they are shared at the top erodes transparency, places a wedge in the relationship between the top and bottom of the organization, and kills trust. Selfishness and self-centeredness also erode trust. Beware of them.

- *Be credible in your actions:* Let your actions align with your words. Walk the talk. When people want to know what you really believe, they look at your behaviors. People will believe you when they see a consistent pattern between your words and your actions. Trust cannot be created if there are inconsistencies between your words and actions. Be reliable and consistent.

- *Let people hold you accountable:* Once you've made a promise, give your people the permission to hold you accountable. And if you cannot meet it, apologize openly to them, explaining why you can't meet it. This should be the exception rather than the norm because if you keep breaking your promises and apologizing every time, you also erode trust.

- *Apologize, if necessary:* If trust is broken, the starting point is to accept responsibility, apologize, and begin afresh.

External

- *Build institutional capability to deliver on your brand promise:* Never make any promise that you do not have the institutional capability to deliver. Be truthful to your customers. Advertisements and promotions might bring customers, but it takes strong systems and processes to deliver on your brand promise to them. While both your ability to attract customers and your capability to deliver on your brand promise are important, I'd advise that you place more premium on your capability to deliver on your promise. Nothing erodes trust faster than the inability to meet the promises you made in advertisements. Remember the oft-repeated cliché in customer service: "Underpromise but overdeliver." To overpromise and underdeliver is a guaranteed strategy of killing trust.

- *Hold your people accountable for delivering on your brand promise:* Once a promise has been made by your organization to its customers, hold your people accountable for delivering on the promise. Give no excuses or explanations for not meeting it. Trust is a perception, and it happens when customers know that the organization will deliver on its brand promise.

- *Seek customer feedback regularly to know whether you are delivering on your brand promise:* How do you know what your customers think if you don't ask them? Don't just ask if they are satisfied; ask specifically for deviations in not keeping with promises made through advertisement.

My Commitment

"I commit to improving the trust level in my team."

Now go ahead and write specific ways to achieve the commitment you've made.

1. _____
2. _____
3. _____

CHAPTER 14

The Six Essentials Every Leader Must Communicate

Communication is the lifeblood of relationships in organizations, a crucial element of the leadership equation.

Want to achieve extraordinary results? Then communicate! Communicate! And communicate some more!

Communication is one of the leader's most important skills for success. Often, leaders get so busy with execution that they fail to communicate their intent and strategic direction; they assume that their people know what is on their minds. The end result is that people are left confused about the direction of the organization and become soothsayers, trying to second-guess the leader's intentions. Just as plants need water and sunlight to grow, communication is the oil of relationships in organizations, a crucial element of the leadership equation. The success or failure of projects or the organization's ability to deliver results is often hinged on communication, effective communication. When this is lacking, gossips and rumormongering reign supreme and sap the energy and vitality in people. The time people should use to focus on achieving results is spent trying to figure out what is happening in the organization. When people need to know and can't find the right source for the information, they make up their own versions and pass them through the grapevine, often to the detriment of the organization.

While this is not a book on communication that teaches the nuances of effective communication—structure, style, choice of words, and so on—I will focus on the essential things a leader must communicate to his people at least once a month. From my research, I believe there are six critical pieces of information that a leader must provide his team at least once every month.

The Six Essentials Every Leader Must Communicate

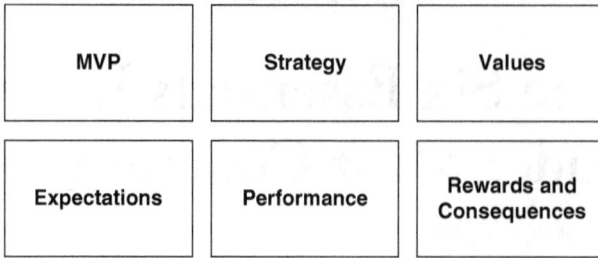

MVP	Strategy	Values
Expectations	Performance	Rewards and Consequences

Figure 14.1 The six foundations of a high-performance communications program

I call them the six foundations of a high-performance communications program (see figure 14.1). I usually advise that each piece be done separately for people to understand them and be done at least once a month. You will be amazed at how many people you think understand this but do not.

MVP

MVP stands for mission, vision, and purpose and I believe it is the first thing every leader should communicate. I am not talking about the generic and often useless mission and vision statements that hang in most corporate head offices, I am referring here to an MVP that connects and resonates with your team because of what really matters to the organization.

Today there is a lot of debate about the exact meaning of those words. Some use mission and purpose interchangeably; others separate them. Some organizations have stopped using mission and vision statements, content to use only one. Whatever you decide to do is fine as along as it is clear and inspiring to your team.

My take is that *purpose* is your overarching reason for being and usually your purpose very rarely changes, if ever. Your purpose is deep and visceral, located someone down in your heart—the fire that stokes within you, the motivations that get you up every morning to make a difference to your world. I call purpose "The Big WHY" or your organizational heartbeat. It is why you wake up in the morning, put in long hours and go the extra mile to create innovative and breakthrough products. It is this *why* that sets great companies and individuals apart from the also-rans.

Your *vision* tells you what you want to become, your dream destination. Your vision is like a noun, a state you want to arrive at, an aspiration. Your *mission* breathes life into your purpose, a verb if you wish. It expresses your purpose in a meaningful way for you and others to relate to it. Your mission answers, "What will be our unique value proposition to our customers and industry?"

As a leader, it is obvious that if you don't communicate your MVP or some variant of it at least once a month, your organization will lose its vitality as people will soon forget why they come to work every day.

Strategy

Your strategy tells you and others where you want to play (and not play) and how you want to play in order to deliver on your MVP and achieve your strategic objectives. It is the unifying theme of how the organization intends to compete and differentiate itself to achieve its objectives. While there are a lot of strategy textbooks that explain the strategy process, I kind of like the simple *who*, *what*, and *how* concepts of strategy I was taught at the London Business School.

Who answers the question of your customer segments or arenas. Who should be your customers? Which customers should your company target and not target? *Everybody* is not an answer or a strategy. You must be crystal clear about who your primary customers are or need to be. Note that I said *primary.* Your primary customers are those customers who will help you to achieve your vision or goal. Your secondary customers are unexpected customers who initially might not fit your primary profile but will purchase your products anyway. Without understanding your primary customers, you do not have a strategy yet. You can define your *who* by market segments and/or by geographic segments.

What explains your product portfolio—your goods and services. What products and services are you going to provide to your identified market segments? And *how* gives the insight into your proposed channels, delivery mechanism (from manufacturing to final delivery to the customer), differentiation strategy, and staging. Your strategy should also clarify where you will not play, what you will not do, and how you will not compete.

Leaders who fail to communicate their strategy to their people will find their people dissipating their energies chasing shadows with little or no results.

To make it practical, your strategy statement must have the following components:

1. Your single strategic objective (use the "from *x* to *y* by *z*" standard)
2. Your identified market segment and potential size, where possible
3. Your product offerings and value proposition

An example of a hypothetical strategy statement using *The HOW of Leadership* could be as follows:

To sell 10,000 copies of *The HOW of Leadership* within the first 12 months of publication by targeting professionals, business leaders, and busy executives around the world who need easily applicable and proven leadership concepts that work.

- *The single strategic objective:* Sell 10,000 copies within the first 12 months of publication.
- *Identified market segment and potential size:* That would be professionals, business leaders, and busy executives around the world (potential size is in millions worldwide).
- *Product offerings: The HOW of Leadership* is in hardback/softback, audio, and e-book formats.
- *Value proposition:* Easily applicable and proven leadership concepts that work.

Another hypothetical example of a strategy statement could be as follows:

To achieve a Return On Equity of 20 percent by 2018 through the provision of mobile banking services that are fast, easy, and convenient to 100,000 rural people who do not have access to traditional financial services.

You can adopt the format for your company, division, or team.

Values

Values are your organization's guiding philosophy as you strive for results. Values answer the following questions: How are we going to behave in the pursuit of our goals? What can we do or not do in the pursuit of business results? What behaviors are acceptable or unacceptable even if results are delivered?

An organization without values is no different from a jungle—a place without rules, where anything and everything is acceptable. In their quest for business results, these organizations have lost their souls. For these organizations, anything is acceptable as long as it makes them look good in terms of the numbers. Ethics and professionalism are thrown out of the window. They are whited sepulchers or walking corpses, and someday, such organizations will come crashing down. Just think of Enron, Arthur Andersen, WorldCom, and Parmalat.

The essence of values is to let your people know that *the means* are as important as *the ends* and that the end doesn't justify the means. The process is as important as the end product. The principles established to guide behaviors are as important, if not more important, as the performance produced. For values to be meaningful, they must aid performance, be measured as part of performance, and become institutionalized.

1. *Aid performance:* The values chosen by the organization must recognize the unique vision of the organization, its history, the uniqueness of its industry and must be the behaviors relevant to help the organization differentiate itself from the competition and achieve sustainable results. Irrespective of the values chosen, as a piece of advice, they must not exceed seven (preferably four to five) with specific behaviors attached to the values. For example, *respect* as a value might have the following behaviors attached: "The use of abusive language in the workplace will not be tolerated" or "We treat everybody equally with dignity irrespective of status, position, sex, or race." Defining the behaviors under each value communicates to employees how the values translate into day-to-day action, thereby avoiding the usual ambiguities about what the values mean and how to apply them.

2. *Be measured as part of performance:* It's now a cliché that what gets measured gets done or people do what they know you will inspect and not what you expect. And if they know that you will inspect their adherence to your organizational values and weigh it as part of their performance appraisal, then it carries more weight. Without measuring compliance to values as part of your performance management process, your values will sound nice but no one will care to obey them. Measurement moves it from the mental "nice to have" to a necessity that stimulates adherence and sustains performance as it becomes cultural.

3. *Be institutionalized:* Institutions have identities that have been shaped by their values. There is a guiding philosophy that transcends any individual or department in the institution. Everyone in the organization is held accountable to living the values. There are no exceptions. The true test of values is how the organization will respond to a high performer who violates one of its core values. It is the true test of what the organization believes in and nothing entrenches values more than the organization's response to such deviations.

Values in Practice: Forte Oil Plc.

When Akin Akinfemiwa was appointed the Group CEO of Forte Oil Plc on December 28, 2011, the company (formerly known as African Petroleum Plc or AP Plc), was in a shambles and morale was low. Having just written off billions in losses as AP Plc, he needed a quick start. After assembling his management team and establishing his vision for the new company, his next major step was a cultural transformation initiative that was hinged on four core values—committed, open, responsive, and respect. These four core values became not just a mantra for the company but the basis for major decisions taken in the company. My partner, Chike Onyia, and I worked with the executive management team to identify the key behaviors under each core value and trained all staff (from the executive management to factory workers) on them. We also designed an appraisal system to measure the adherence to the core values. People who failed to adhere to the core values even after coaching were asked to resign and some were even fired. All the goals the company set for the first three years have been met and some exceeded. This was due in part to the core values initiatives of the Group CEO. Core values and cultural transformation initiatives, when done right, help organizations achieve breakthrough results.

Expectations

Expectations refer to what each person must contribute to the organizational results. It breaks the strategy into operational and tactical plans with assignments of key roles and responsibilities. Like in a football team, to win the game, the strikers must score, the midfielders must provide the assistance, the defenders and keeper must prevent the opponent from scoring. Each person makes a contribution to the overall success of the team.

Expectations must be clearly communicated to all and agreed by all, and people need to be constantly reminded of their deliverables. A critical part of expectation management is communicating your beliefs about your team. It's one thing to set targets; it's another thing to let your people know that you believe in their abilities to achieve the targets. The Pygmalion in management concept teaches us that the manager's expectations will become self-fulfilling prophecies, that people become what the most significant people in their lives expect them to be. And the significant people in the lives of an individual are his parents, spouse, and supervisor. Wow! *As a leader, you play a significant role in the lives of your staff.* And guess what? By the time they enter the workplace, their parents' role has reduced considerably, and the leader's role is now the most important factor determining behaviors and results. Isn't it amazing that you have in your hands the power to shape your people's destiny for good?

Believing in someone is staking a claim on that individual's future. If you do not believe in your people's futures, there is no way you can inspire confidence in them. So, take a minute and answer this simple question honestly about every person in your team: What do I really believe about each person in my team?

Note that I asked what you *really believe* about each person? I mean what you believe deep down in your heart about each person. And how do you know what you really believe about someone? Watch your *internal conversations* about the person—the things you say to yourself about the person that nobody hears. Be honest and write everything down and have the courage to discuss it with the person; do so for each member of your team. And if you are finding it hard to believe something good about a member of your team, then you need to be honest about it and call the person for a meeting. Say to the person, "I am trying hard to believe the best of you, but you have given me so many reasons not to. Help me change that perception." But if you don't believe in any member of your team, then you need help! Go for professional counseling.

Positive expectations by you as the leader expressed in words and deeds will unlock the potential of your followers to achieve great results, while negative expectations expressed in words and deeds too will become the cap that limits their achievements. The power of expectation is expressed through your beliefs about that person. That is, what you believe to be true is usually what happens. Positively communicate expectations and beliefs together.

Performance

This is the actual result produced by each person. Expectation points to what people are supposed to do and can do; performance points to what they have done or are doing. Expectation is forward looking; performance is backward looking. People need to know how they are doing, and great leaders do not wait for formal appraisal days to tell their people how they are doing. They provide regular, timely, specific, and constructive feedback about their team's performance.

- *Regularity* deals with the frequency of feedback—which should be a minimum of once a month.
- *Timeliness* deals with when to provide it—usually when you catch your people doing something great or not so great. That is, it should be an on-the-spot feedback.
- *Specificity* deals with addressing the issues—no vague or ambiguous feedback. If you adopt the timeliness nature of feedback, you will always be specific because you are addressing issues as they happen.
- *Constructiveness* deals with the goal of feedback—to help the person continue to do the right things or change for the better. Feedback is different from criticism. Criticism points to mistakes without providing solutions. Feedback provides solutions to mistakes.

Criticism destroys confidence; feedback builds confidence. Criticism takes the wind out of your team's sails; feedback is the gust of wind that enables them to fly. Effective feedback acknowledges problems, provides solutions, and encourages actions needed to change. Provide constructive feedback constantly.

Rewards and Consequences

All behaviors have payoffs. We are creatures of habit. People are usually motivated to avoid pain (consequences) or to experience pleasure (rewards). When and where there is no pain for negative behavior or no pleasure for positive behavior, people usually become complacent and settle into perpetuating negative behaviors. Leaders must constantly use the right motivational approach including the use positive reinforcement and inducements to encourage high performers, and when necessary, apply negative reinforcement to discourage poor performers.

Field Guide to Help You Get Started on Communicating the Six Essentials

Ask your team the following questions:

I. Mission, vision, and purpose
- Why are we here? Why was the organization established?
- What exactly are we trying to accomplish?
- Where are we headed? What is our ultimate destination?
- How do we know when we get there?

II. Strategy
- Do you know our strategy for achieving our vision?
- Do you think our strategy will help us to achieve our vision?
- Are we structured in a way that will help us to achieve our vision?

III. Values
- What do we stand for? How are we different from the other organizations in our industry?
- Are we, especially our leaders, living up to our espoused values?
- Are there known deviations from our values that have not been addressed?

IV. Expectations
  ○ Do you know what is expected of you?
  ○ On a scale of 1 to 10, how confident are you of your ability to achieve your performance targets?
  ○ Do you know that I believe in your ability to achieve your goals and am willing to provide you with any support or assistance you need to achieve them?

V. Performance
  ○ How are you doing in line with your targets?
  ○ What is working/not working?
  ○ What challenges are you currently facing?
  ○ What support do you think you need to achieve your targets?

VI. Rewards and sanctions
  ○ Are you motivated by the organizational rewards to achieve your performance targets?
  ○ Do you know what the sanctions are for not achieving your goals?
  ○ Is the organization fair in its application of rewards and sanctions?

Just before You Begin

In communicating the six essentials, think through the following:

- *Who*—recipient/audience: To whom is the communication addressed? What is his or their motivations, fears, likely objections? Without matching your message to your audience, that message is likely not to make the desired impact.
- *Why*—the purpose: Can you summarize the objective in a sentence? Why is the message important?
- *What*—the content and behaviors expected: This is not only the specific points you want to communicate but also the changes you want to see happen because of the communication. What do you expect them to do thereafter?
- *Where*—the location: Where is the best place to make the announcement? Why did Martin Luther King Jr. choose the Lincoln Memorial as the place for his "I Have a Dream" speech? Location matters!

- *When*—the timing: When is the best time to communicate the message? The right message at the wrong time will not have the desired impact.
- *How*—the strategy: How you intend to present your case or evidence. Consider structure, style—stories, anecdotes, rich personal examples and medium (tools).

Thinking through these will help dramatically improve your communication effectiveness.

My Commitment

"I commit to ensuring that I communicate the six foundations of a high-performance communications program monthly."

Now go ahead and write specific ways to achieve the commitment you've made.

1. _____

2. _____

3. _____

CHAPTER 15

Open the Channels
of Communication Upward,
Downward, and Across

Upward communication is a win-win situation. Staff are free to express themselves and feel that they are being heard, while managers can use the information gathered to create buy in. I don't see what a leader will lose by encouraging it.

Want to achieve extraordinary results? Then open the channels of communication in your organization!

In the previous chapter, we noted that communication is the lifeblood of organizations. The conversational environment determines to a large extent the culture of the organization, which directly affects performance. We are safe to say that there is an indirect link between the nature of dialogue in an organization and the performance of the organization. To improve performance, therefore, leaders must open the channels of communication and allow information to flow freely upward, downward, and across the organization. While the previous chapter focused mainly on information flowing downward from the leader to the staff, this chapter focuses on communication flowing upward and across.

Upward Communication

Upward communication is becoming more popular in today's organizations. As organizations face increasing competitive pressures and changing customer demands, speed is becoming the new differentiator in today's business landscape. What customers want today are results delivered in a timely manner and with a friendly attitude. Customers are so much under pressure themselves and so much in a hurry that they will not forgive any organization that will not respond to their needs on time. Responding quickly to changing customer needs means that organizations must break down the walls of bureaucracy to allow the free flow of information from employees interfacing with customers to corporate headquarters for quick decision making and back to them for speedy implementation.

When Paul O'Neill became the CEO of Aluminum Company of America (or Alcoa, as it was known in 1987), his vision to turn around the struggling company was anchored on one keystone habit—safety. To make his vision actionable, he instituted the 24-hour rule, where all injuries in the factories must be reported to the corporate headquarters within 24 hours. This 24-hour rule forced the company to break down the barriers of bureaucracy because it required foremen to report such injuries to their supervisors, who would then report them to their VPs, who in turn would report them to corporate headquarters, all within 24 hours. By creating the 24-hour rule and making it mandatory, he got information to flow freely upward. Executives who did not obey the rule were fired. The company was able to institute a lot of changes to meet the zero-injury safety goal as a result of the flow of information upward. By the time O'Neill stepped down in 2000, Alcoa's market value had increased from $3 billion in 1986 to $27.53 billion in 2000, while net income had increased from $200 million to $1.484 billion.[2]

Executives like Paul O'Neill know that upward communication can aid in the following:

- *Unleash the spirit of innovation and creativity in the organization:* People who work in the trenches or interface with customers know customer needs better and can suggest a lot of ways of improving the service delivered to customers if only they are asked. Without creating an environment where people who interface with customers or work in the trenches can report observations and proffer solutions, the organization will not unlock the wealth of innovative ideas in the minds of their people. Sometimes innovation happens not by thinking out of the box but by simply asking workers in the trenches what they feel can be done to improve the current products and services being rendered to customers.

- *Help top management know issues affecting subordinates:* Without upward communication, managers will assume that they know the issues affecting their people. Only by creating the avenue where people can speak up will management know what their people's issues are and what is driving their behaviors. And until leaders understand the belief systems—the motivations and payoffs—driving the current behaviors within the system, there is not a chance in the world that they can create lasting change. One key to influencing people is not only by expressing your views about their desired future but also by listening to their challenges.

- *Create buy in from subordinates for decisions reached by management.* Usually, when people play a part in the decision-making process, even when the final decision is different from their own, they feel more obligated to accept the decision. However, if they are not involved in the process and decisions are handed down by executive fiat, resistance will be higher. This means that involvement usually leads to acceptance and buy in and increases engagement. To get buy in to your plans, you need to find a way of involving people in the decision-making process.

Make It Safe and Worthwhile

One thing I have noticed about leadership is that you cannot mandate free agents to do anything against their will. They must want to do it before they will do it. Little wonder that Dwight D. Eisenhower defined *leadership* as "the art of getting someone else to do something you want done because he wants to do it." If he doesn't want to do it, chances are that he won't do it except he is forced to—which is not leadership but dictatorship. In the same manner, leaders cannot mandate upward communication. They can only motivate and encourage their constituents to speak up. For this to happen, leaders must do four things.

Go First

The leader must demonstrate the commitment toward people speaking up. People will only speak up when they feel important and appreciated.

The leader's responsibility here is to let his team know that their opinions count. The leader must seek out information from his people. If he doesn't encourage it, people will not speak up.

Make It Safe for People to Speak Up

People will only speak up when they feel safe or believe that the leader will not use their views against them. Until you make people feel safe and not attack their opinions or justify your current behaviors, people won't speak up. Sometimes people look at how you have treated others with contrary views in the past before they will speak up in the present. If they feel that others were not treated fairly or that their opinions were discounted or were shot at, they will not speak up. Make it safe for your people to speak up. If you find that you want to disagree with their position, hold it. What you do at such moments, called critical incidences, will determine whether people will be free to speak up again.

Make It Worthwhile and Meaningful

Making it worthwhile means that the leader must show his people that he is willing to implement the suggestions that are within his control. Coincidentally, the day I wrote the initial draft of this chapter, I had a meeting with about 40 of my leaders. After we went through the basics (i.e., what we are doing well and what we can do better), some issues were raised, one of which was the need for friendliness in the organization. Some felt that the bond of togetherness is gradually slipping away and noted that we need to bond more with one another. After listening to all the suggestions about how to improve bonding and camaraderie in the organization, I immediately implemented one of the suggestions by calling for a 5-minute break and asked the 40 leaders to go around and meet someone that they didn't really know and get to know the person. You could immediately feel the energy in the room. After the initial 5 minutes, I had a struggle stopping them. That action communicated to them that I would implement suggestions on matters within my control immediately, where possible. Make it worthwhile and meaningful by letting people know that you are willing to listen and implement some of their ideas on matters that are within your control.

Listen Effectively

Nothing kills speaking up faster than the attitude that says, "I know it all. That's a stupid idea. What are you even saying?" Your inability to listen without being defensive will destroy the spirit of open communication that you are trying to institute. In "The Sound of the Forest," a parable of leadership by W. Chan Kim and Renée Mauborgne, the authors wrote about a king who sent his son to an ancient master to learn the basics of being a good ruler.

The assignment that the master gave the prince was to go to the forest for one year, after which he should return and describe the sounds he had heard in the forest. He went, listened to superficial sounds, returned, and narrated his experience. The master sent him back to listen more attentively. Surprised by the master's request, he went back, and after sitting still for a while, he heard the sounds the master wanted him to hear, and he returned with excitement and described the sounds to the master.

The master replied,

> To hear the unheard is a necessary discipline to be a good ruler. The demise of states comes when leaders listen only to superficial words and not penetrate deeply into the souls of the people to hear their true opinions, feelings, and desires.[3]

Listening effectively is a necessary skill of great leaders. Someone once said that the reason God gave us two ears and one mouth is so that we can listen twice as much as we speak. But to some leaders, it is as if God gave them more than one mouth and no ears. They are always speaking even when it is not necessary; consequently, they lose the respect of their team.

The truth is that listening is not an easy skill. The average person desires to be in control even when it is not necessary making listening a major challenge for many. However, listening is a skill that must be learned if we must become better leaders. Here's three disciplines we must practice if we are to listen attentively:

- *Have presence of mind:* The literal meaning of "to listen" is to "pay attention to." So when you are listening, you are paying attention to only one thing—the person speaking. Presence of mind is the ability to focus on the listener. It is to be physically and emotionally present. Most leaders are distracted when their followers begin to speak. They allow their minds to wander, shoot e-mails, take calls, and so on. The superficial reason for being distracted is that they are busy; the deeper reason is that they don't value the person standing in front of them that much because if you truly value someone, you give that person your undivided attention. Being present is a skill that great leaders have and that their followers appreciate. Being present is the present we give to people when they are in our presence. Next time your associate or colleague walks up to you to talk, be present!

- *Suspend judgment:* Being present is the first part of listening, but suspending judgment is the next most important skill of a good listener. Don't jump to conclusions and assume that you know where the person is headed when you have not listened effectively. Leaders have a high need to seek closure on issues. Because they are pressed for time and have too many things calling for their attention, they want to achieve closure quickly and jump to the next thing. But doing so sends a wrong message to the team. Seeking closure when you have not listened effectively is amateurish. Sometimes you need to keep an open mind because seeking closure too early can cut the flow of information the next time and can lead to disastrous effects. And guess what? You are not omniscient—the all-knowing one. Leaders who feel they know it all and have heard it all reveal how little they know and lose the respect of their followers.

- *Understand emotional viewpoints:* Go beyond superficial words to understand the emotional viewpoints of your people. Guess what? Listening effectively doesn't mean you have to agree with their viewpoints but requires you to first understand them and then not criticize them for it. That is, even when you don't agree with their viewpoints, be easy on criticism. At least appreciate the fact that it was important enough for that individual (or the team) to speak up. Be easy on arguments and criticism. Don't hurt their emotions or make them feel stupid just to prove how wrong they are. How you handle dissenting views or possible disagreements will go a long way in determining whether your team will speak up the next time. You are the leader, and people expect you to act maturely, especially with dissenting views from others. One hallmark of maturity is the ability to listen to and hold contrary opinions without being defensive or attacking the other person. You may be correct, yes, but please do not attack the other person!

Tolerance is the spirit of true leadership. True leaders accept contrary opinions gracefully without feeling threatened or wielding the big stick.

Listening Effectively: Pay Attention to This Triad

What should leaders pay attention to as they begin to listen to their people and open the channels of communication upward? Just as in "The Sound of the Forest," where the future leader was advised to hear the unheard, I advise leaders to pay attention to these three factors as captured in Figure 15.1:

The Dominant Internal Conversations within the Organization

What are the general words used to describe the organization? If I ask your people to describe what it feels like to work in your organization

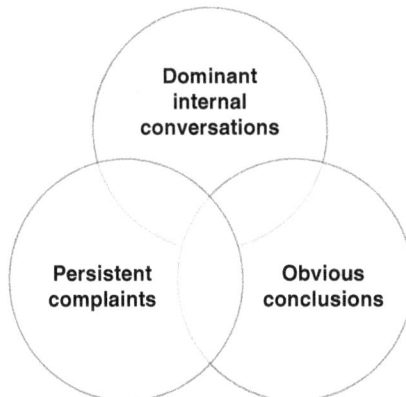

Figure 15.1 A leader's listening triad

in one word or a sentence, what will the common thread be? The common thread is the dominant internal conversations in your organization. It is what your people are saying about your organization and your leadership behind your back, the silent whispers. Usually, the dominant internal conversations are heard two to three levels below you. As an executive, you will not hear the dominant internal conversations from your direct reports. To hear these conversations, you need to go two levels below. Why is it important to hear them? Because the dominant internal conversations determine the level of people's engagement with the company. If the dominant conversations are "Management doesn't listen" or "There is no job security here" or "We are slaves," what do you think will be the level of employee engagement? You get the idea.

The Persistent Complaints

What are the issues that they have against the organization? If you ask your people "What are the most common challenges within the organization affecting your ability to do a great job?" you will get their persistent complaints—for example, "Our internal processes are too slow," "There is no cooperation between the various departments," "There is no trust."

Obvious Conclusions (Assumptions and Mindsets)

What far-reaching conclusions have they made about the management team and the organization? If you ask your people what they believe to be true about the management team and the future of the organization, you will get their obvious conclusions. The dominant conversations and the persistent complaints will form their obvious conclusions— for example, "This organization is confused about its strategic intent," "They are not serious about achieving business goals," "This is a great place to work."

Dangers to Avoid

The goal of opening the channels of communication is to hear the unheard but whispered throughout the organization. However, in opening the channels of communication, leaders should avoid the following:

- The negative practice of gossip
- The tendency to seek out only those who will tell them what they want to hear and not what they need to hear
- The tendency to show disapproval or punish those who are vocal enough to tell the leader their sincere opinions even if those hurt

Creating an environment where upward communication occurs makes it easier for lateral communication among teams to take place. Lateral communication fosters team spirit and coordination of tasks and helps in stimulating creativity and innovation.

My Commitment

"I commit to improving on my listening skills and creating a safe environment for upward communication in my team or organization."

Now go ahead and write specific ways to achieve the commitment you've made.

1. _____
2. _____
3. _____

CHAPTER 16

Focus on Excellence
in Execution

*No matter how beautiful the strategy, you should occasionally look at
the results.*

—Winston Churchill

Want to achieve extraordinary results? Then focus your attention on
excellent execution!

It was the largest ship afloat in the world when it was commissioned.
It got its name because of its size. Its maiden voyage was with pomp and
pageantry from Southampton, the United Kingdom, to New York, the
United States. Yet it never arrived at its destination. On April 15, 1912,
the RMS *Titanic* sank in the North Atlantic Ocean after colliding with an
iceberg, leading to the loss of over 1,500 lives. On June 2, 2015, another
cruise ship, the *Eastern Star* (a Chinese cruise ship), went down during a
storm. Over 400 senior citizens died.[4]

While vision points to your destination, strategy to the process, and
engagement to your people's commitment toward organizational success,
execution is the glue that binds all together, without which disasters like
the *Titanic* and *Eastern Star* will become a daily occurrence.

Execution is the new bride in strategic thinking today. While organizational failures due to poor execution do not lead to sudden death like
the *Titanic*, think of the impact of the wasted resources, the demoralizing
effect of the closure of factories, and the loss of jobs that happen due
to the failure of an organization to execute. Think of all the beautiful,
well-bounded, and expensive strategic plans that have been thrown into

the dustbin of history because of the failure to execute. In such organizations, morale plummets, staff become cynical to another strategic plan, and anxiety over the future increases.

Different authors have put the average success rate of most strategic plans between 30 and 60 percent. That is, at best, only 60 percent of companies will achieve their strategic goals for the year; at worst, 30 percent. Looking at it in another way, at best, only 60 percent of their strategic plans will be realized by most companies. Using this method, whatever your strategic goals are for the year, multiply it by a factor of 0.6 (at best); that's what you are likely to achieve. And in the worst-case scenario, multiply it by 0.3; that's what you might achieve. The reason? Poor execution. This is perhaps why Ram Charan and Geoffrey Colvin estimate that bad execution accounts for 70 percent of the reasons CEOs fail.[5]

Therefore, getting execution right can be the difference between having a job and being shown the door as a leader, and it can double your performance and make you look like a star.

Why Execution Fails

Execution fails for many reasons. The most common reasons can be subdivided into four categories as captured in Figure 16.1:

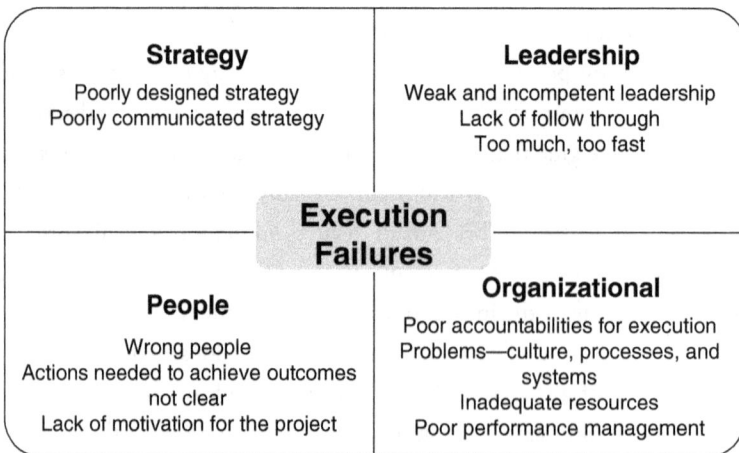

Strategy	Leadership
Poorly designed strategy Poorly communicated strategy	Weak and incompetent leadership Lack of follow through Too much, too fast
Execution Failures	
People Wrong people Actions needed to achieve outcomes not clear Lack of motivation for the project	**Organizational** Poor accountabilities for execution Problems—culture, processes, and systems Inadequate resources Poor performance management

Figure 16.1 Common causes why execution fails

Strategy

- *Poorly designed strategy:* Execution is as good as the thinking and assumptions behind the design and formulation of the strategy. To say that strategic thinking is obsolete, and execution is king, is akin to saying that the captain is more important than the ship. Both the ship (strategy in this case) and the captain (execution) are important. One cannot do without the other. The Titanic failed because it was poorly constructed (strategy) and had an obstinate captain (execution). A good strategy without execution will take you nowhere. And good execution of a poorly designed strategy will take you to the port of disaster. The advice that Peter F. Drucker gave in 1963 is relevant even today. He said, "There is nothing quite so useless as doing with great efficiency something that should not be done at all."[6] Good execution begins with good strategy. A brilliant execution of a bad strategy is no better than a good strategy that was poorly executed as the organization would waste resources and manpower in both cases.
- *Poorly communicated strategy:* When people do not know the strategic direction of the company and the expectations based on the strategy, that strategy will not be executed properly.

People

- *The wrong people:* Execution boils down to one thing—people. Execution is as good as the people who will implement it. To attempt to execute an A-rated project with an organization filled with C-rated people is a daydream and a recipe for disaster.
- *Actions needed to achieve outcomes not clear:* When people do not know what exactly they need to do in order to achieve the company's strategic goals, then execution is bound to fail. Call it leverage behaviors or keystone habits, people need to be clear about the steps they need to take to achieve the goals set by the company. Strategic direction must be broken down into actionable behaviors.
- *Lack of motivation for the project:* When people are not motivated about the project, execution will fail. It takes competent people who are highly motivated to execute projects brilliantly. They must want a stake in the success of the project for the project to succeed.

Organizational

- *Poor accountabilities for execution:* Whose responsibility is it to ensure that the deliverables are met? Does the company have a monitoring program to ensure that assigned tasks are delivered? When people know that the company doesn't take results seriously, then it doesn't matter how fantastic the speeches the leaders give about the new direction of the company are, they will not give their best to execute it efficiently.

- *Organizational problems—culture, processes, and systems:* Organizational culture and processes work in tandem to either help or hinder execution. A broken culture with silo mentality, turf protection, and political fiefdom is a sure guarantee that the strategy will end up in a black hole. Processes enable how things get done in the organization. Projects are delivered through organizational processes. Without fixing broken processes, execution will be a mirage. Great leaders tweak both their organizational culture and their processes to align them with their visions and enable their people to execute.

- *Inadequate availability of resources:* Sometimes execution fails because the people who will execute the strategy do not have the resources (organizational tools, authority, and skills) to perform the task. No amount of motivational mantra will enable such people to win in the marketplace without the availability of resources.

- *Poor performance management.* It's now a cliché that what gets measured gets done. If they know that you will not check if your instructions were properly executed and not reward those who carry out the instructions and hold accountable those who don't, they will not execute their assignments. Failure to institute a rigorous performance management system is a common reason for execution failure.

Leadership

- *Weak and incompetent leadership:* Weak, ineffective, and incompetent leadership is another major reason that execution fails. When leaders cannot hold robust dialogue about the strategic intent and objectives of their organizations and do not show the commitment expected to pull the initiatives through, execution is as good as dead.

- *Lack of follow through:* It is the specific job of leadership to follow through to ensure that work is done. When the leader fails to follow through, results will not be achieved.

- *Too much, too fast:* When leaders introduce a series of changes atop one another too quickly, their people will suffer from what I call *execution fatigue.* Some leaders equate activity or busyness with productivity. They are restless. They are always looking for the next big thing. They derive joy from moving from one project to another and doing too many projects at the same time. What they don't realize is that there is a limit to what people can do per time. Each project exacts people's physical, mental, and emotional energies and depletes their reservoir. So, although the leader may be busting with energy, his people will burn out and drop the ball in a crucial project if he doesn't give them the time to catch their breath and replenish their energy levels.

Improving Excellence in Execution

By addressing each category/factor, you can improve your chances of execution success.

Strategy

- *Robust and sound strategy:* Have robust dialogue with key stakeholders during the strategy formulation stage. The goal here is not agreement first but dissent first. Divergent thinking should be encouraged before convergent thinking. Since execution is only as good as the thinking that produced the strategy, you should ensure that the strategy is robust and sound, and sound strategy usually emerges after heated and rigorous debate about the direction of the company. Groupthink is a recipe for execution disasters. Be wary of your strategy where everybody is singing its praise and does not question the strategic objectives or the rationale behind it or have any reservations about it. As Matthew S. Olson and Derek van Bever noted in *Stall Points: Most Companies Stop Growing, Yours Doesn't Have To,* "The greatest threat to a company's growth is posed by obsolete strategic assumptions that undermine market position, and by breakdowns in innovation and talent management."

- *Communicate the strategy:* Use every means (face-to-face, e-mail, video recording, and so on) to communicate your strategy. Don't be afraid of over communicating it. More projects fail from under communication than from over communication. Vary the means and methods of communicating your message to avoid understanding fatigue. Use case studies, stories, change agents, and so to get the message across. Be creative in your thinking. Get feedback from your people to test their understanding. Ask them to share with you what's working and what's not working and what they think the company can do to change the situation.

People

- *The right people:* Get the right people behind major projects. Consider their attitude, motivation, capacity, and discipline. Attitude is the foundation, motivation is their willingness to be a part of the project, capacity is the ability to execute, and discipline is the willingness to follow through to ensure that the project is completed with excellence. These four qualities are pivotal in execution. Capacity alone is not sufficient. Without the right attitude, a person will have problems with his teammates. Without motivation, he will not be committed. And without discipline, he will not follow through.
- *Clarify the actions needed to achieve outcomes:* Clarify the steps to take. Begin by asking yourself and your people, "What is the one thing we must do daily that will have the greatest impact on our organizational goals?" If they cannot tell you the one thing they must do (or at best not more than two to three steps they must take), then the actions needed to achieve the outcomes are not yet clear. *Execution* is actually a borrowed military term, and just thinking about the word *execute* means that there must be an object to execute and the *how* to execute it. Therefore, if your people do not know the *how* to execute the plan, then it doesn't matter if they know the target. However, ensure that the actions are realistic and feasible. Nothing kills motivation and execution faster than unrealistic actions.
- *Motivate people:* So crucial is motivating people that a chapter (chapter 10) is dedicated to it.

Organizational

- *Establish accountabilities for execution:* Execution must be broken down into individual responsibilities, and each individual held accountable (see Chapter 17, which is on holding people accountable).

- *Institute the right culture and design the right processes:* In the 2008 article published in Harvard Management Update "Creating and Sustaining a Winning Culture" by Paul Meehan et al., the authors wrote, "Strategy matters—sure. But without a winning culture to drive it forward, your strategy is taking you nowhere." In the Fall of 2013 Harvard Business Review OnPoint magazine on How to Create a Culture of Excellence, the HBR editors concluded that "what top-notch companies have that mediocre companies lack is a culture of excellence—beliefs and behaviors demonstrated day in and day out that enable and inspire everyone in the organization to do their best." Culture matters in execution. The results you want should determine the culture you institute and the processes you design. *Culture* is often defined as "how you do things," and how you do things is often reflected in your processes and systems. Fix both your culture and processes. Tweak the culture constantly to drive the results you want. Review organizational processes to ensure that they enable your people to execute. How do you know your processes will support your ability to execute? Think of the three characteristics of world-class processes: *simplicity* (easy to understand), *speed* (quick response to customer needs), and *flexibility* (the ability to adapt to changing customer needs). Strive for simplicity, speed, and flexibility in your processes. The opposites are organizational complexity, delays, and rigidity—the three destroyers of an organization's ability to execute.

- *Provide resources:* Provide the resources necessary for your people to succeed but teach them to be creative. Resource leverage is more important than just resource availability. To leverage resources, they should develop an entrepreneurial mindset to maximizing existing resources even if it means moving resources away from nonproductive businesses to productive ones, or trading resources with other teams within the organization in order to succeed.

- *Rigorous performance management:* Institute a rigorous performance management system to reward excellence in execution.

Leadership

- *Strong leadership:* Provide visible leadership. Show commitment to the execution phase. Vary your leadership style to match the execution stage. Be the change and execution champion. Communicate effectively. Demonstrate charisma. Make results nonnegotiable.
- *Follow through:* Inspect daily, weekly, and monthly. Use focus and discipline to get people to do the things that are necessary. I'd like to change one word in Winston Churchill's quote at the start of this chapter: "No matter how beautiful the strategy, you should [always] look at the results." Always look at the results. Nothing else matters without it.
- *Pace Projects:* Don't jump from one project to another. Rotate project teams where possible. Don't burden the same people over and over again. Execution requires more physical, mental, and emotional energy than planning. Projects can be planned in one day but take months to execute. Don't confuse the sweetness of planning with the sweat of execution. Don't underestimate the work required because decisions were reached within an hour. Execution requires people to roll up their sleeves and be in the trenches. Give your people a break to catch their breath before announcing the next big thing. Doing too many things at the same time is a sign of poor leadership. Your people will conclude that you are confused. Don't try to change too many things too fast, especially if you are a new leader. For every leader who changed too many things too fast and succeeded, there were hundreds who tried and failed. Don't add to the statistics of execution failures.

Improving Execution Questionnaire

Here is my simple execution questionnaire for you to use to gauge the readiness of your team or organization to execute:

	Restraining forces					Driving forces				
Strategy	-5	-4	-3	-2	-1	+1	+2	+3	+4	+5
1. The organization has a clear strategy to WIN in the marketplace, one that exploits our unique strengths and weakens our competitors' strengths in the marketplace.										
2. Strategy has been communicated from the C-Suite to the front lines using different means and is constantly being reinforced.										
3. There is clear understanding and buy in by majority into the strategy.										
4. Strategy is realistic and scalable—there is a general belief that it is achievable.										
5. The timing is RIGHT. There's no better time to pursue the strategy than now as market conditions are in our favor.										

	Restraining forces					Driving forces				
People	-5	-4	-3	-2	-1	+1	+2	+3	+4	+5
1. Our people have the capacity to execute our strategy. They are constantly trained to meet the ever-changing customer demands.										
2. They are clear about their responsibilities and the actions they need to take to execute the strategy.										
3. They are motivated to execute our strategy because incentives are aligned with their execution/interests.										
4. People feel empowered to take necessary steps/decisions to achieve organizational goals.										
5. Our recruitment process targets people who fit the profiles required on the basis of our strategic intent.										

(continued)

	Restraining forces						Driving forces				
Organizational	−5	−4	−3	−2	−1	+1	+2	+3	+4	+5
1. There are clear accountabilities established for execution—who does what, when, and how.										
2. The organizational culture (values, norms, beliefs, and behaviors) and structure aid execution.										
3. We have best-in-class processes to support execution—speed, simplicity, and flexibility.										
4. Resources and tools are allocated effectively to help execute the strategy. There is alignment of all business units with the strategy.										
5. There is a clear, transparent, and rigorous performance management framework in place.										

	Restraining forces						Driving forces				
Leadership	−5	−4	−3	−2	−1	+1	+2	+3	+4	+5
1. Leaders of the company provide visible leadership and show commitment to the execution of projects.										
2. They use the appropriate leadership styles and vary them when necessary to achieve the desired results.										
3. They follow through and provide necessary support to ensure that projects are executed.										
4. They pace projects appropriately to ensure completion before moving to the next big thing.										
5. They hold people accountable—demand answers, ask tough questions, reward performance, and sanction poor performance.										

© Improving Execution Questionnaire, Dr Maxwell Ubah.

My Commitment

"I commit to working on improving the execution capabilities of my team."

Now go ahead and write specific ways to achieve the commitment you've made.

1. _____

2. _____

3. _____

CHAPTER 17

Hold Your People Accountable for Results

An accountable environment does not accept excuses for nonperformance and does not give people the opportunity to trade blames and pass the buck. At the "account table," only results matter, not excuses!

Leaders achieve results through people. They have a relentless focus on results. And they achieve results by holding themselves and their people accountable. Without the discipline of accountability, results will remain an illusion. The ability to hold people accountable and institute the discipline of accountability throughout the organization is one key difference between great leaders and ordinary, mediocre leaders. Great leaders hold their people accountable for results; ordinary leaders, on the other hand, accept excuses for nonperformance from their people.

What exactly is accountability? Figure 17.1 shows a simple accountability chart:

At the center of accountability is responsibility—assigned tasks and expectations concerning results. The attitudes of the staff and the organization toward results are seen at the opposite ends of the spectrum. I have noticed that organizations enthrone either one of the two as you cannot have accountability for results and excuses for nonperformance at the same time—they are mutually exclusive.

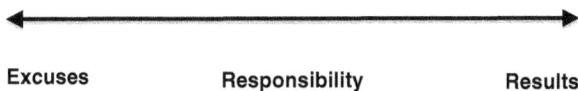

Excuses   Responsibility   Results

Figure 17.1 The accountability chart

To understand accountability, look at the opposite ends of the spectrum. Where accountability is absent, people give excuses and get away with nonperformance. Excuses make people blame others for their personal failures. The goal of excuses is to absolve oneself of complicity and make mediocrity acceptable and respectable. When managers allow people to give excuses, their people begin to trade blames and finger-point others as the reason for their failure. They blame everything and everybody except themselves. And like George Washington Carver observed, "Ninety-nine per cent of failures come from people who have a habit of making excuses." What they seek is sympathy, understanding, and respect for nonperformance. When allowed to thrive, it creates a culture that strangulates performance.

Accountability, on the other hand, is different. It means that excuses will not be accepted for nonperformance. *Accountability is the discipline that ensures that assigned tasks are completed on time and as expected—no excuses, trading blames, or passing the buck.* With the discipline of account- ability, performance reigns supreme. A simple way to look at the meaning of the word *accountable* is to break it into two components: *account* and *table.* So, holding people *accountable* is like setting up a table where people must give account of the stewardship of their time, resources, and efforts. When people know that there is no table or that they can come to the table and are not expected to give account or won't be held *account- able,* they dissipate their energies in frivolities and waste organizational resources at their disposal. But when they know that they will be held accountable, they become disciplined and dedicated to their tasks.

The discipline of accountability is the only remedy for people giving excuses and trading blames. An accountable environment does not accept excuses for nonperformance and does not give people the opportunity to trade blames and pass the buck. At the "account table," only results matter, not excuses!

And guess what? Nothing is more motivating that knowing that you work for an organization where results matter! Weak leaders think that instituting a culture of accountability for results will scare people away, but they are mistaken. Without the culture of accountability, high performers will become discouraged and leave and you will be left with mediocre staff. Just like ants are attracted to sugar, high performers are attracted to a culture of accountability for results.

Building Accountability into Performance Expectations

One of the primary tasks of leadership is achieving results. And achieving results is impossible without the discipline of accountability. But how do leaders build accountability into their organizations?

The process of accountability can be broken down into four steps as shown in Figure 17.2:

Clarifying Performance Expectations

If people do not know what they need to give account for, how can you hold them accountable? The discipline of accountability begins with clarifying performance expectations. A clear sense of responsibility is the starting point of accountability. Here's where a lot of leaders make the mistake (from my experience as a leadership coach). They sit down at corporate head office and decide on the goals for the year and announce it to all the staff. Often, the employees are left wondering how the goals were arrived at. This is perhaps the most crucial stage in the accountability process. Get it wrong, and you can as well forget about the outcomes.

The leader's primary responsibility here is to get buy in for the goals of the team, both from a task and an emotional perspective. To get buy in, the leader must be willing to listen to the concerns and fears of his people about the targets and address them accordingly, not dismiss them. When

Figure 17.2 The accountability process

leaders are dismissive of people's concerns, they too become dismissive of the leader's aspirations. There will be no alignment or goal congruence.

This step requires that you communicate, clarify, and get buy in for performance expectations. What follows is my simple performance contract guide designed to help you communicate, clarify, and get buy in for your performance expectations. You can adapt it as appropriate in your organization.

A *Performance Contract Chart*

Name of employee:	Job title:
Department:	Date:
	Description
Performance expected and why	
Process input or action plans (behaviors expected)	
Problems anticipated (skill gap, more manpower, changing economic conditions, and so on)	
Provisions made (training and development opportunities, support, empowerment, and so on)	
Progress report (frequency and format)	
Rewards/consequences	
Signatories	Employee: Manager:

This chart leaves no room for ambiguities about the performance expected, but the most important benefit of this chart is that it helps you to identify potential problems and address the employee's concerns, thereby helping you in reaching agreement faster with the employee and getting buy in.

Encouraging Action and Initiative

Communicating and clarifying performance expectations is the starting point of instituting the culture of accountability. The next step in the accountability process is to encourage action and initiative as people sometimes do not do what they know they should do. How do you encourage action and initiative?

This is achieved through regular follow-through sessions. You need to check in frequently with your team to see how they are progressing with the assigned task. Regular follow-through sessions will help you identify and quickly nip problems in the bud. The sessions will also enable you to put contingency and performance improvement plans in place and on time.

Leaders who are surprised at the results of their staff simply show that they did not follow through in the discipline of accountability. Your goal as a leader is not to be taken by surprise with respect to poor performance. This will only happen (i.e., not being taken by surprise) when you conduct regular follow-through sessions.

And regular follow-through sessions are particularly necessary in the following situations:

- *Critical tasks:* If the task is critical, then you can't afford to be taken by surprise. You need to conduct regular follow-through sessions.
- *New employee:* If the employee is new and you are not yet sure of his capabilities, then you ought to conduct more follow-through sessions in addition to coaching.
- *Challenging task:* If the task requires people to put in extra hours or deliver on a major project within a short time frame, then you need to conduct more regular follow through.

At the follow-through sessions, please ask the following questions:

- What did we agree that you will accomplish? (This is to get his/ their understanding of the task.)
- What is the progress report? (This is to find out what actions they have taken, if any.)
- What are the results and/or challenges? (This is to know the results so far or the challenges being experienced on the way.)
- What do you need to do to ensure that you complete the task and achieve the expected results? (This is to ascertain their knowledge about all the steps necessary to deliver the results.)

Providing Support and Feedback

Accountability, by its very nature, is not one directional. Most times, when people talk about accountability, they describe it as a top–down approach. Accountability is both top–down and bottom–up. Accountability is mutual. To achieve results, the manager has a part to play. To assign tasks without providing the required support in terms of feedback, coaching, encouragement, and organizational resources is simply the abdication of responsibility. To demand results without providing the needed support is witch hunt.

The manager must ask himself constantly, "What do my people require from me in order to meet their targets? Have I done everything I need to do to ensure that they achieve their goals?" Organizational leaders must also ask the same questions: "What do they require from us?" and "Have we done everything we need to do for them to achieve their goals?"

To expect results without providing support is akin to expecting to catch a whale in a pond or to expect the delivery of a baby without conception.

In bottom–up accountability, the staff must also hold their managers and organizations accountable for providing the support and tools necessary for results. They should ask and even demand for the support they need. To assume that your manager knows everything you need to succeed without you asking is stupidity, plain and simple.

In bottom–up accountability, you cannot use the nonavailability of resources as an excuse. Accountable people do not wait for their leaders to provide the resources; they take the initiative and follow through with their managers until they get the resources they need to deliver the results. No excuses!

Reviewing Performance

This is the final step of accountability—to settle accounts with your people. There are two methods at the leader's disposal: the performance evaluation and the performance appraisal processes (Chapter 19). Performance evaluation is the informal evaluation of performance and should happen regularly and frequently. This should be done at the end of every accountability cycle or at least once a month. The goal is to identify if performance targets were achieved and what developmental plans, if necessary, should be put in place for the employee. Performance appraisal usually happens once or twice a year. It is a formal process that reviews performance over that period, and is used for rewards, promotions, and compensation purposes.

Here are some questions to get you started with the performance evaluation process:

- What was the performance expected versus the performance realized?
- How does this measure up to what you know the employee can produce?
- Is there a potential–performance gap? And if so, why? Is it a problem of knowledge, motivation, resources or even challenges beyond their control?
- What developmental strategy is required to bridge the gap?

Without the discipline of accountability, results will continue to be a mirage. You are paid as a leader to deliver results. Accountability is the discipline that guarantees great results. Begin to practice it today!

My Commitment

"I commit to becoming a more accountable leader, holding myself and my team accountable for performance results."

Now go ahead and write specific ways to achieve the commitment you've made.

1. _____
2. _____
3. _____

CHAPTER 18

Question-Based Leadership

Great leaders lead with questions. Great leadership is not about providing all the right answers but about asking all the right questions. A genius knows all the right answers; a leader, all the right questions.

One of the greatest skills in the repertoire of a leader is the ability to lead with questions. Yes, you heard me right. The ability to ask the right questions is perhaps the sine qua non of great leaders, and it differentiates them from mediocre leaders.

A genius knows all the right answers; a leader asks all the right questions; a fool thinks he knows all the right answers. You are either one of the three: a genius, a leader, or a fool.

Most often, when leaders want to communicate vision, motivate staff, gain alignment, and correct performance challenges, they use one or two strategies. They either *tell* (informing people what to do) or *sell* (persuading people to change) and often leave the most potent toolkit in their leadership bag: the ability to ask questions, the right questions.

Consider the following example: James is facing some challenges meeting his targets. Over the last one month, James has become disengaged and is no longer interested in the job.

Strategy 1: Tell (and Sometimes Yell)

Warn James that if he doesn't improve his performance, he will be fired.

Comment: This strategy will obviously not work because James is already disengaged. At this stage, threats and sanctions will not produce the desired results because James doesn't care any longer.

Strategy 2: Sell

Explain to James why he needs to become engaged and take his work seriously. Tell James he can do it and you believe in him (motivational mantra).

Comment: While this strategy is better than the first one, it still does not address James's issues. Why did he become disengaged in the first place? What really happened? This well-meaning strategy will not achieve the desired results because the main issues have not been addressed.

Strategy 3: Question

Ask James what his challenges are. Why was there a sudden change in his performance? What are the key factors?

Without probing, the manager will not know why James is disengaged. Perhaps he was not promoted or has been sidelined by his manager. Is he at the receiving end of a conspiracy of the other teammates? Or is he having personal issues to deal with, whether physical, mental, or emotional?

Even after finding out the answer, the manager should resist the temptation to tell and/or sell. He should use the same method with James and ask him, "So how do you think we should resolve this issue or overcome this challenge?" Let him proffer the solutions. The manager can then ask, "What commitments will you make to improve your performance going forward?" and/or "What assistance do you need from me to help you overcome the challenge?"

Note that James identified the problem himself, proffered the solution(s), and made commitments toward resolving the problem. James owns the process; the manager or leader is just a guide. And this is the original concept of leadership—to guide people to achieve their own personal greatness.

The Benefits of Using the Question-Based Approach

Reveals Collective Understanding or Common Knowledge

One often repeated mistake of leadership is to confuse information with understanding. Just because a leader has sent a memo, an e-mail, or even had a face-to-face meeting with his people and explained his vision and strategy doesn't mean the people understand them. The leader leaves with a feeling of accomplishment of having had a successful meeting, while the followers leave with a feeling of confusion—they still do not get it. Asking questions bridges this gap and gives the leader the insight into the collective understanding of his people and helps him adapt his strategy appropriately. The next time you have a meeting with your people, rather than explain the vision, ask your people, "What exactly are we trying to do as an organization?" You will be surprised at the diversity of answers that they will provide. Now you understand why alignment is impossible. Until people have a unified understanding about goals, they cannot be aligned to a common purpose.

Unearths Frustrations

One of the most important responsibilities of leadership is the ability to manage the energy of their followers to achieve the desired results. Energy management is one of the leader's primary tasks. Leaders must ensure that energy is not dissipated in petty quarrels, organizational silo thinking, selfish interests, and so on. The difference between world-class organizations and the also-rans is simply this: World-class organizations focus all their energies on achieving world-class results, while mediocre organizations dissipate their energies in frivolities, politics, petty quarrels, and organizational silo thinking among others. Until leaders ask, "What is not working?" "What systems and processes are hindrances to our performance?" they will never know the frustrations of their people, unearth tons of innovative ideas, or achieve breakthrough results. Asking the right questions is the key to transforming any organization. As a leader, until you know the frustrations of your people and make a conscious effort to remove the hindrances or reduce their frustrations, you will not unleash the energy within your workforce and experience a quantum leap in performance. But it all begins with the courage to ask the right questions.

Shifts Focus and Changes Behaviors

The holy grail of motivation is to shift people's behaviors. However, studies have shown that nothing achieves a shift in motivation and people engagement faster than giving people the ownership of the discovery process. People are usually more motivated by their own discoveries and decisions than decisions passed on to them from the top. That's why the tell and sell approaches often fails to achieve the desired shift in behaviors. A closer look shows that the word *question* can be broken into two: *quest* and *ion*. A quest is an expedition, a desire for something, while an ion is an electrically charged particle. *Questions set the mind on a quest, an expedition, a pursuit that ultimately shapes behaviors.* Asking the question, "How can we improve our performance or reduce cost or beat the competition?" will set the minds of your people to constantly think of new ways to achieve your organization's business goals. Look at it this way: When you ask positive questions, you are challenging them to a "fight." It is another way of communicating to them that you trust them to come up with the answers, and it is often the elixir necessary to transform ordinary people to become history makers.

Why Some Leaders Don't Use the Question-Based Approach

If the answer to getting people motivated, aligning them toward a vision, and achieving a quantum leap in performance is asking the right questions, why don't leaders use this tool? The answers are not farfetched.

- *They don't know any better:* Here the leader is sincere but doesn't know about the question-based approach to getting feedback and creating alignment.
- *They don't have the time:* Leaders are under so much pressure and using the questioning toolkit requires that leaders are patient with their staff in the face of performance challenges. It is easier to just tell and yell and go on to the next project on the agenda than spend time questioning their staff about issues.
- *They think they know all the answers:* Positional leadership sometimes creates the illusions that make leaders think that they are infallible (cannot make mistakes), omnipresent (can be everywhere at the same time), omniscient (know it all), and omnipotent (can

do everything). These illusions make morons of leaders who fall for them. Because they think that they know it all, they make decisions they think are the right decisions but are perceived as morons by their people because they know that the decisions are wrong. Take James, for example. His reason for disengagement might be that the manager is not walking the talk or living up to the organizational values, but the manager thinks that James is not engaged because he is not serious or has attitude problems. When leaders think that they know all the answers, they usually reveal their ignorance, because they don't.

- *They are afraid of the answers they may get:* Sometimes leaders are afraid of asking the right questions because they are afraid of the answers they may get. Why ask what's not working and hear the plethora of problems that point directly at your failures? It is a lot easier to assume you know, play the ostrich, and plod ahead—often to the destruction of the organization. It takes maturity to hear what you need to hear. Leaders often fail not because of lack of passion or charisma but because they fail to hear the unheard but spoken throughout the organization (see chapter 15). To really get to the heart of any issue, go beyond your direct reports to the people at the front line or people two steps below you, and don't be afraid of what you will hear.

Every major progress in life and in business began with a new set of questions. Legend has it that Isaac Newton asked a question about what made an apple fall from a tree and the law of gravity was discovered. Albert Einstein asked a question about people's interpretation of their experiences, and the theory of relativity was discovered. NASA asked what it would take to put a man on the moon and return him safely, and a new vista of space exploration was opened. Steve Jobs asked a question about how to simplify the user experience in the mobile phone space, and the iPhone was the result. To change your experience, you need to change the questions you ask yourself and your team consistently. To change your corporate destiny, you need to change your conversational environment by asking the right questions.

My Commitment

"I commit to leading with questions."

Now go ahead and write specific ways to achieve the commitment you've made.

1. _____
2. _____
3. _____

CHAPTER 19

Judge Performance Accurately

High performers are motivated by recognition for work done. Without recognizing them, you create a culture of mediocrity and empower average and poor performers to take over your organization.

Leaders must be thorough when it comes to judging performance. We have defined leadership as relationships × results. Results matter in the leadership equation. In fact, the final test of a good leader is results. Did he improve the personal effectiveness of his individual players? Did he produce results? Did he make the organization or state better? Every year managers and coaches are fired in the English premiership. Why? Because of poor results. If leaders are judged by results, then they should also judge the results being produced by their teams accurately—no sentiments.

To judge performance accurately, leaders need to understand the performance management process. A simple performance management process is shown in Figure 19.1.

Effective performance management begins with setting goals and objectives for the year with clear action plans. Goals are usually long term and possibly generic in nature—for example, to become a leading player in your industry is a goal. Objectives are short to medium term, specific in nature, and support your goal. So, the objective might be to sell 100,000 units of a specific product monthly or quarterly as the case may be.

Leaders know that to achieve the results, people must put in effort. To put in effort, people must be motivated, so leaders must spend time motivating their people to put in the effort required to achieve results. But effort alone doesn't guarantee results. It is intelligent, sustained, and skillful effort that guarantees results. Therefore, leaders must coach

Figure 19.1 A simple performance management process

and develop the capacity of their people in order to achieve the results. However, having motivated, coached, and developed their capacity, leaders must play the role of conducting both performance evaluation and performance appraisal objectively.

As explained in Chapter 17, which is on holding people account-able, performance evaluation is usually done to improve the abilities of the individual and should be done regularly, while performance appraisal should be done once or twice a year. This segment focuses on the perfor-mance appraisal portion as the performance evaluation and coaching of staff have been covered earlier.

Purpose of Performance Appraisal

The goal of performance appraisal is to agree on the achievements of the staff with a view to determining the rewards (promotions or bonuses) and development needs (further training, coaching, or counseling) or appro-priate sanctions, where necessary. The questions the leader and the staff must answer during the performance appraisal process are as follows:

- What was agreed at the outset?
- Did the staff achieve it?

- To what degree?
- And what should be the recommendations based on the achievement?

To answer these questions objectively, three things are necessary:

- *Clear goals* must have been communicated and agreed upfront between the manager and the employee.
- *Regular coaching* and *feedback sessions* are held with the employee during the performance cycle for him to know how well he is doing and to avoid surprises during appraisal.
- *Documentary evidence* is available. The facts should speak for themselves. Performance appraisal should be as objective as possible. The performance cycle is usually six months, so keep your critical or significant incidence file to use to judge performance accurately.

What Should We Measure?

In agreeing on performance goals, the organization must determine what to measure. It should focus not only on business results (performance) but also on the behaviors of the people (attitudes/values). To what degree should it focus on both dimensions? Here the battle line is drawn between quantitative and qualitative measures. I believe both are important, but whether you decide to do 80–20 or 50-–50 is irrelevant, in my opinion.

What is important is that the weighing scale and metrics you adopt must capture both the results achieved by your people and their alignment with your organizational core values, and managers and staff must be clear about the measures. Often, I see organizations that pride themselves on their values but do not measure them in performance appraisals. In such organizations, there will be a lot of deviations from the corporate values as people will focus more on business results at the expense of their behaviors and interactions with one another. If people are rewarded in some way for not keeping the organizational values, then your value statement should be thrown out of the window as it doesn't mean anything in your organization.

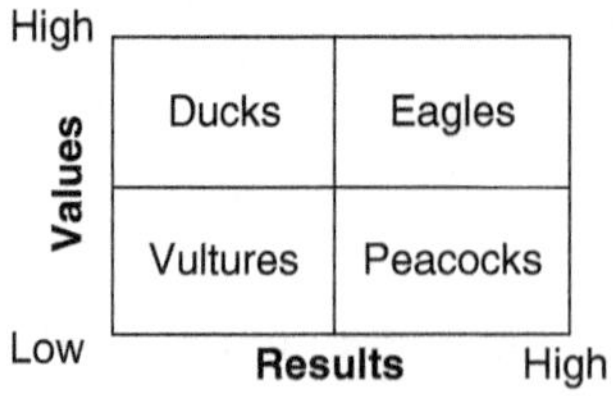

Figure 19.2 The results–values performance matrix

Your performance appraisal scale should have clear solutions and recommendations for the following categories of staff:

1. People who achieve results and abide by your corporate values
2. People who achieve results but do not abide by your corporate values
3. People who do not achieve results but abide by your corporate values
4. People who do not achieve results and do not abide by the values

Using the results–values matrix, the four categories of staff are as shown in Figure 19.2.

Eagles and vultures are easy to deal with. The challenge is with peacocks and ducks. If values are not measured, peacocks will be rated as superstars even though they are the antithesis of what the organization stands for, and if values carry more weight, ducks will score high even though they are poor or mediocre. Getting the balance right is critical. My recommendation would be that you make it impossible for anyone to score an A without adherence to your core values.

Eagles

They are your star performers. They are classified into two:

- *Consistent performers:* They meet between 80 and 100 percent of targets regularly and do not require much encouragement to get things done. They are self-starters and should be rewarded with bonuses and promotions when necessary.
- *Stars:* They are punching above their weight and usually exceed 100 percent of assigned targets. They should be placed on a fast

career growth path and not burdened with problematic, lagging, or average staff. However, if they fail to live up to the company's values, they should be treated as peacocks.

Vultures

They have both performance and interpersonal problems. They consistently fail to meet assigned targets even after coaching has been provided and do not abide by the organizational values. They are high-maintenance staff. Like vultures who feed on carcasses, this group feeds on problems—they are troublemakers. They are toxic to the system and should be asked to resign.

Peacocks

These are individuals who can be counted upon to achieve results, but they have problems abiding by the organizational core values or in their people (interpersonal) skills. I think the starting point in dealing with peacocks is to diagnose the problem and place them on a personal improvement plan, and watch. If they fail to change, they should be asked to resign like the vultures.

There are three reasons why peacocks are the way they are:

- *Genetic makeup and traits or personality:* They are the classic type A personality—aggressive, competitive, impatient, strong willed, highly opinionated, and so on—just like Michael in Chapter 1.
- *Ignorance:* Sometimes the violations by peacocks are due to the fact that the only model they have about achieving results is one of aggressiveness and riding roughshod over others. That's what others did to achieve results, and that's what has worked for them in the past. For them, it is the only way they know to achieve results. The Machiavellian mindset of "the end justifies the means" holds true for them. They believe that eggs must be broken to make an omelet. Therefore, like a bulldog, they are ready to bulldoze anyone who stands in their way of achieving results.
- *Stubbornness:* Stubbornness is when the person has refused to change even after the destruction he leaves in the wake of achieving

the results has been pointed out. Their personal philosophy is that you must accept them the way they are with all their baggage.

How do you deal with peacocks?

- *Recognize the cause:* personality, ignorance, or stubbornness.
- *Provide adequate feedback:* Sometimes peacocks are oblivious of the damage they have caused or are causing. In providing feedback, use the classic sandwich approach: Praise them for results, point to the problems, and end with your confidence in their ability to overcome the challenges.
- *Challenge their pride:* Peacocks believe that they can conquer the universe. Use their ego and pride as the fuel to drive them to change. Let them see that the violations do not reflect who they claim to be.
- *Design a workable improvement plan, including training and coaching:* Irish novelist Oliver Goldsmith observed that "people seldom improve when they have no other model but themselves to copy." Peacocks need to be shown a different method of achieving results. In their minds, they know of only one way, and it is working. What they need is a better way to achieve the same results.
- *Gracefully exit:* If the peacock is still stubborn after all the intervention, then you must ask him to resign or let him go because, by allowing him to remain in the system, your organization has surrendered its leadership to him. No individual is bigger than an organization no matter the results he is contributing if he is destroying your corporate values. If he doesn't believe in what you believe in, then why is he a part of your organization?

Ducks

They are the opposite of peacocks. They embody your organizational values but struggle with business results. Like eagles, we can divide ducks into two:

- *Laggards:* These are people who meet 20 to 40 percent of the assigned targets. More on-the-job coaching is recommended, but failure to improve performance should lead to termination of appointment.

- *Average:* They meet 50 to 60 percent of assigned targets regularly. If average is due to capacity, then place them on a slow-growth career path. If average is due to motivation, then motivate. Do not fire this group. There will always be noncritical jobs that they can handle. Eagles are demotivated by noncritical jobs, which the ducks should handle. But if average slips to lagging, then place them on probation and exit if performance doesn't improve back to normal.

Biases to Avoid When Judging Performance

Leaders must be objective when judging performance because crucial decisions are taken on the basis of the performance ratings of an employee by the manager. Therefore, leaders and managers should ensure that the appraisal ratings are without bias. The most common biases are as follows:

Halo

This is the tendency to overrate an employee because of certain qualities in the employee. For example, someone is known to be hardworking and hits his numbers consistently. The quarter he doesn't meet his numbers, he is still given a good grade because he is known to be hardworking. Or someone hits his numbers consistently but is a bully and has poor working relationships with others, but because he hits his numbers, all his sins are forgiven. Halo bias can also occur in the following situations: good working relationships between the manager and employee, same ethnoreligious affiliations, recommendations from someone at the top, or an employee subservient to the manager's whims and caprices.

Horns

This is the opposite of halo. While in halo bias the employee can never do anything wrong, in horns, the employee can never do anything right. The opposite of the factors that cause halo effect can cause horns effect. For example, if an employee is an excellent performer but doesn't play a subservient role to a manager who wants it, he might be rated unfairly.

Recency

The focus here is on the last thing that the person did just before the review session, making it the basis for judging the whole appraisal period. For example, a poor performer pulls a last-minute deal, and he is rated excellently well, or a good performer makes a mistake just before the appraisal, and nothing else matters.

Strict

Nobody can get an A even if you meet 100 percent of your target. A is reserved for deities, and since you are not one, you can't get an A no matter how good your grade is.

Same Band

Everybody gets the same rating in the team irrespective of their individual contributions.

Comparison

Here is where the organization rates people not on the basis of their absolute performance but on the basis of what others on the same grade achieved. People are usually put in a basket or band, and their results compared. For example, it doesn't matter if your score is 90 percent, if more than 5 percent of the class scored above 90 percent, then your grade is a B. Your final score is always relative to others in your band.

Shifting Goalpost

Here is where the organization keeps shifting the targets set for their staff such that the appraisee doesn't really know what the basis for appraisal is. Oftentimes, the appraisee only knows about the new measures a week to the new appraisal date, and as such, can do nothing about it.

To soar, an organization needs to be filled with eagles. Without judging performance accurately, you demotivate your eagles, who either fly to other high-performing environments or lose their wings in your environment, and you are left with vultures and ducks and a few peacocks, who lord it over the rest. High performers are motivated by recognition for work done. Without recognizing them, you create a culture of mediocrity and empower average performers to take over your company.

Case Study: ABC Ventures

The company has a poor record of retaining high potentials, and the CEO is worried about the high staff turnover in his company. Investigations reveal that internal promotions and transfers were based on the CEO's mood rather than on competence or merit. (The CEO doesn't understand why such high potentials can't stay with the company even though the company pays relatively well compared with its competitors.) To be successful, majority of the remaining workforce are busy jostling to curry his favor rather than working to get the job done. Which of the performance biases are at work at ABC Ventures?

My Commitment

"I commit to judging performance accurately."

Now go ahead and write specific ways to achieve the commitment you've made.

1. _____
2. _____
3. _____

CHAPTER 20

X-Ray Successes and Failures and Institutionalize Lessons

Those who fail to learn from the mistakes of the past condemn themselves to repeating the same errors.

Real leadership is a batting average—sometimes you win, sometimes you lose. While we have established that leadership is relationships × results, we, however, know that sometimes the route to success is not linear. It has detours and contours on the way marked by failures and challenges. Sometimes the seeds of failure are sown during times of success and vice versa. That is, success can lead to failure, and failure can birth success. Success might look better than failure at the beginning but can become the carrier of failure at the end. What is important in your leadership journey is not just success or failure per se but the lessons you are learning from both. I believe one of the goals of leadership development is openness and maturity—to learn from both success and failure and institutionalize the lessons learnt. Organizations that treat failure as an orphan and success as a king will miss valuable lessons from both.

From Success to Failure—Common Causes

For some individuals and organizations, their successes actually led to their downfall. From my years of research, Figure 20.1 is my chart to explain the downfall from success to failure for many an individual and many a company.

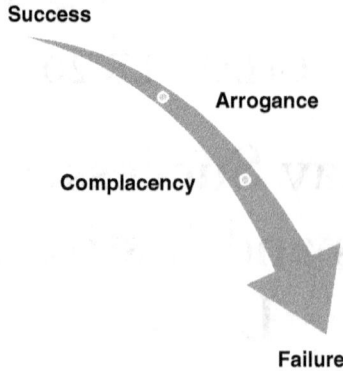

Figure 20.1 From organizational success to failure

Success

Here the company is doing great, leading the market, and breaking new grounds with record profits. The company has so many awards to show for its innovative products and services. Customers love the company's products and are addicted to them. They can't seem to do without the company and its products, at least, for the time being.

Arrogance

This happens when the company begins to believe in its own success stories. It begins to think that its customers do not have a choice but to do business with it. "Our customers are here to stay," the management team say to themselves. "Where else could they possibly go? They cannot leave us for newer entrants. Our competitors are just wasting their time." Arrogance or what I call "The No One but Us" syndrome is the end result of such faulty thinking process.

Arrogance manifests in three ways:

- *Ignoring changing customer needs:* Because the company's management believes that its customers will always be loyal to the organization, it takes them for granted and ignore their changing needs and tastes. The proverbial statement by Henry Ford that "a customer can have any color of car that he wants as long as it is black" begins to play out. The customers are given a "take it or leave it" proposition. The delusion of thinking that its customers will remain loyal irrespective of the quality of the service is the height of arrogance. At this stage of arrogance, the company feels that it is doing its customers a favor, that its customers should consider it a privilege doing business with the organization, and that with or without its current customers, it will succeed. It will isolate the few disgruntled customers and point to the millions still doing business with it. The company's management turns the advice of Peter F. Drucker that "the purpose of a company is to create a customer" on its head to mean that the purpose of the customer is to serve the company.

- *Ignoring competition:* At the stage of arrogance, the company says to itself,

> We are still the leader, the numero uno of our industry. Other players might be trying to enter to steal a share of the market, but wait a minute, we are still number one! Business is still very good, and market share is growing, so ignore the competition. Let's leave the small players to be innovative. We have the big customers, so they can have the small customers and experiment with newer products.

- *Ego investments without rigorous debate:* Here is the delusional belief that because the company is successful in one area, it can expand into other areas and displace the incumbents there. Usually, a company becomes successful by debating its strategies, doing market research, targeting customers with innovative products, and so on. But with success comes hubris and the false belief that success in one area will translate into success in other areas. The company begins to stretch itself thin, dreams up ego projects outside its core competencies, and announces to the world that it is going to take the market from the incumbents in new markets in a few months. Aggressive acquisition, diversification into unrelated industries, and the craze for going global even against the evidence to the contrary are three common manifestations of this disease. Rigorous debate is thrown outside. Staff who are bold enough to challenge the assumptions are attacked. Dissenters are seen as devils and not fit to be part of the organization. The end result is usually destruction of shareholder value.

Complacency

Complacency is the natural result of arrogance. An arrogant company doesn't see the need to respond to competitive changes in the marketplace, and by the time it wakes up, it is sometimes too late to address them. Blockbuster, Atari, Nitel, BlackBerry are some notable examples.

Failure

This is the end result of complacency, but like the story of IBM, which tethered on the brink of bankruptcy in the early 1990s and bounced back, all hope is not lost. A company can hit rock bottom and bounce back if it applies a disciplined approach to dealing with the problem.

Lessons from Success—Arresting the Downward Slide

Humility and Hunger

Success is more dangerous than failure, for while failure lets you know that you still have a lot of work to do, success tends to make you feel that you have arrived at your destination. Success is a poor teacher; it blinds you to hubris. To overcome the hubris that success can cause, you need to be humble (not be carried away by your successes) and hungry (seek new grounds). Never lose the fire within because of success. Humility and hunger are the antidotes to the dangers of arrogance and complacency caused by success. Follow the advice of Steve Jobs when he told the graduating students from Stanford University during his commencement speech: "Stay hungry, stay foolish!"

Institutionalize Lessons

For success to have any lasting impact, companies must institutionalize lessons learned from it. Why did we succeed? What exactly did we do to succeed? How can we replicate our success? Turn the organization into a case study and allow your people to debate why the organization succeeded and what lessons can be learned from its successes.

Marshall Goldsmith, in the book *What Got You Here Won't Get You There,* introduced two powerful concepts: "because of" and "in spite of". He explained that people are successful "because of" certain things they did right and "in spite of" all the things they did wrong. He noted that trouble begins when people confuse the two or think that they are successful "because of" their "in spite of". For example, a bully who achieved results might be tempted to think that his bullying contributed to the results—because of—when he achieved the results in spite of his bullying. You get the idea. In the same manner, your organizational success is due to all the things you did right and in spite of all the things you didn't do right. Do not confuse the two.

As you debrief, find out your "because of" (the things that you did so well) and also all your "in spite of" (the things that you did not do well). Without identifying the two, chances are high that you will plod ahead, thinking that you will always be successful in spite of your obvious weaknesses. When the industry changes or an aggressive new competitor enters your market space, your weaknesses will become the limiting and crucial factor. So, challenge your people to think not only of your strengths but also of your weaknesses, and institutionalize the lessons.

Also, you can institutionalize lessons by looking at individuals within the organization who are succeeding despite the odds and use them as case studies. If they are succeeding in the same environment where others are failing, such individuals should be studied to share what they are doing differently, and their behaviors should be extracted and institutionalized. But don't confuse the "because of" with the "in spite of". Turn your organization into a corporate university by learning not just from textbooks but also from internal practitioners who are applying certain principles with tangible results.

Begin Search for the Next Opportunity

Successful companies begin to search for the next wave of opportunity before it becomes apparent. They maximize today's opportunities and markets while looking for tomorrow's opportunities and markets. And once they find tomorrow's opportunities, they begin the journey toward maximizing them even when today's business opportunities are still making money. Failures wait to maximize all of today's business opportunities before committing to search for tomorrow's business opportunities only to find out that the opportunities are long gone. Successful organizations cannibalize their own products by replacing them with new and better products instead of allowing the competition to do so.

Expand with Care

Success boosts organizational confidence, which sometimes blindsides even well-meaning executives into thinking they can take on the world, often to disastrous effects. Expansion into new categories should be done after rigorous debate.

Lessons from Failures

Companies fail for common reasons. When I took the Managing Corporate Turnarounds course at the London Business School, some of the common causes we identified for corporate failures included the following:

1. Poor strategy
2. Failure of corporate governance
3. Failure to retain top talent
4. Weak internal processes and corporate governance issues
5. Poor-quality products and services
6. Weak market demand
7. Intense competition
8. Cash flow challenges and capital inadequacy issues
9. Poor leadership
10. Wrong mergers and acquisitions

A closer look reveals that most of the factors listed are internal factors. I think they can be divided broadly into four—leadership, people, idea and strategy, and culture and execution (including systems and structures)—all of which have been covered in relevant sections of this book.

In learning from failures, just ask four questions:

1. *Leadership:* Corporate failures usually begin at the top. Is the leadership of the organization the appropriate leadership given the peculiar challenges and opportunities that the organization is facing? It takes strong, courageous, and decisive leadership to maximize today's business opportunities and navigate the murky waters of hypercompetition.

2. *People:* Success without the right people is like a sperm without the ovum. Conception happens when the right sperm (the leadership) meets the right ovum (the people). Ask, did we have the right people in place? Were they aligned with the vision of the organization?

3. *Idea and strategy:* In winning organizations, there is a fit between the view of their competencies, external opportunities, and the unique value they create for customers. Failure results when one of the three is absent. Ask, is the idea of the business the right one? Was it designed to maximize our view of the world, capitalize on our strengths, and deliver unique value to our customers? Sometimes failure happens when there is a misalignment of the who, what, and how of the strategy—that is, targeting the wrong customer segment (who) or challenges with the features of the product (what) or a problem with the distribution (how).

4. *Culture and execution:* The importance of culture cannot be overemphasized. Remember that I likened the leader to a sperm and the people to an ovum. But the fertilized ovum must be implanted in the uterus for a baby to be born. Fertilization without implantation is useless. For the baby to be carried to term, the right uterine environment, supported by the mother's overall well-being, is necessary. Organizational culture is akin to the right uterine environment and the mother's overall well-being. Without the right culture, strategy is dead on arrival. Ask, did we have the right culture in place to support our execution capabilities? Did our systems, structure, and processes support our strategy or hinder it?

My Commitment

"I commit to ensuring that my organization or team learns from its successes and failures."

Now go ahead and write specific ways to achieve the commitment you've made.

1. _____

2. _____

3. _____

Notes

Section 1

1. Wharton. 2004. Becoming the Best: What You Can Learn from the 25 Most Influential Leaders of Our Times. http://knowledge. wharton.upenn.edu/article/becoming-the-best-what-you-can-learn-from-the-25-most-influential-leaders-of-our-times

2. *Advanced English Dictionary on Microsoft Store*, copyright © 2015, Cosmos Chong.

3. Prov. 28:16, Holman Christian Standard Bible®, Copyright © 1999, 2000, 2002, 2003, 2009 by Holman Bible Publishers.

4. Berkun, S. n.d. https://leadershiplicks.com/2016/12/13/i-think-that-2/

5. Grove, A. 1998. *Only the Paranoid Survive: How to Exploit the Crisis Points.* New York, NY: Crown Business.

6. Ibid.

7. Wikiquote. n.d. https://en.wikiquote.org/wiki/Abraham Lincoln

8. Stanford News. June 14, 2005. "'You've got to find what you love,' Jobs says." *Stanford News.* http://news.stanford.edu/news/2005/june15/ jobs-061505.html

9. https://www.nytimes.com/2002/09/06/business/will-justice-department-go-after-dunlap.html

10. https://www.cnbc.com/2009/04/30/Portfolios-Worst-American-CEOs-of-All-Time.html?slide=6

11. Waldrop, M.M. n.d. "Dee Hock on Management." *Fast company.* http://www.fastcompany.com/27454/dee-hock-management

Section 2

1. Proust, M. n.d. "Marcel Proust Quotes." *Brainyquote.* http://www .brainyquote.com/quotes/quotes/m/marcelprou107111.html

2. Smith, C. 2015. "Video: Celebrate 8 Years of iPhone With This Hilarious Blast From Steve Ballmer's Past." *BGR.* http://bgr .com/2015/06/29/steve-ballmer-laughing-iphone-video

3. http://tonyelumelufoundation.org/africapitalisminstitute/about-us/what-is-africapitalism/

4. Tzu, L. n.d. "Quotable Quote." *Goodreads*. http://www.goodreads.com/quotes/10627-to-lead-people-walk-beside-them-as-for-the

5. Crabtree, S. October 8, 2013. "Worldwide, 13% of Employees Are Engaged at Work." http://news.gallup.com/poll/165269/worldwide-employees-engaged-work.aspx

6. Ibid.

7. Ibid.

Section 3

1. Reuters. October 22, 2015. "Volkswagen CEO Says Emissions Scandal Bill Could Rise." *CNBC*. http://www.cnbc.com/2015/10/22/emissions-scandal-volkswagen-may-have-to-set-aside-more-funds-if-sales-fall.html

2. C. Duhigg. 2013. *The Power of Habit: Why We Do What We Do and How to Change* (New York City, NY: Random Books).

3. W.C. Kim, and R. Mauborgne. 1992. "Parables of Leadership." *Harvard Business Review*. https://hbr.org/1992/07/parables-of-leadership

4. S. Varandani. "Yangtze Cruise Ship Disaster: China Gathers 60 Specialists To Probe Eastern Star Sinking." *International Business Times*. http://www.ibtimes.com/yangtze-cruise-ship-disaster-china-gathers-60-specialists-probe-eastern-star-sinking-1960096

5. http://archive.fortune.com/magazines/fortune/fortune_archive/2002/05/27/323712/index.htm

6. P.F. Drucker. n.d. "Quotable Quote." *Goodreads*. http://www.goodreads.com/quotes/29838-there-is-nothing-quite-so-useless-as-doing-with-great

About the Author

Dr. Maxwell Ubah, CEO of Strategy House, is a highly sought after leadership coach in Nigeria and a leading leadership voice in Africa. He is a graduate of the Sloan Fellows Program in leadership and strategy from the London Business School. He has helped thousands of executives at different stages in their personal leadership journey to improve their leadership effectiveness. Using simple but powerful concepts, Dr. Ubah helps individuals to identify their leadership challenges and discover steps to overcome them with powerful and transformational results.

His core competencies are in leadership and people development, change management design and implementation, strategy formulation and execution, organizational culture assessments and interventions, and organizational performance optimization.

He has conducted leadership training programs for various reputable organizations across different sectors in Nigeria with excellent ratings. He has also facilitated leadership training in Ghana, Senegal, Zambia, Kenya, Cameroun, Dubai and Côte d'Ivoire.

He is the author of *Seven Great Life Lessons: Powerful Strategies for Reaching Your Goals* and *The Difference: What Successful People Know and Do That Ordinary People Do Not*

He can be reached at

Twitter: @maxubah

e-mail: mubah@strategyhouseng.com

Mobile: +234-802-323-3321

Index

OTHER TITLES IN THE HUMAN RESOURCE MANAGEMENT AND ORGANIZATIONAL BEHAVIOR COLLECTION

- *Managing Organizational Change: The Measurable Benefits of Applied iOCM* by Linda C. Mattingly
- *Creating the Accountability Culture: The Science of Life Changing Leadership* by Yvonne Thompson
- *The 360 Degree CEO: Generating Profits While Leading and Living with Passion and* Principles by Lorraine A. Moore
- *Conflict and Leadership: How to Harness the Power of Conflict to Create Better Leaders and Build Thriving Teams* by Christian Muntean
- *Precision Recruitment Skills: How to Find the Right Person For the Right Job, the First Time* by Rod Matthews
- *Practical Performance Improvement: How to Be an Exceptional People Manager* by Rod Matthews
- *Creating Leadership: How to Change Hippos Into Gazelles* by Philip Goodwin and Tony Page
- *Organizational Design in Business: A New Alternative for a Complex World* by Carrie Foster
- *Magnificent Leadership: Transform Uncertainty, Transcend Circumstance, Claim the Future* by Sarah Levitt
- *Power Quotes: For Life, Business, and Leadership* by Danai Krokou
- *Negotiating with Winning Words: Dialogue and Skills to Help You Come Out Ahead in Any Business Negotiation* by Michael Schatzki
- *Conflict First Aid: How to Stop Personality Clashes and Disputes from Damaging You or Your Organization* by Nancy Radford
- *Slow Down to Speed Up: Lead, Succeed, and Thrive in a 24/7 World* by Liz Bywater
- *The Challenge to Be and Not to Do: How to Manage Your Career and Maximize Your Potential* by Carrie Foster

Announcing the Business Expert Press Digital Library

Concise e-books business students need for classroom and research

This book can also be purchased in an e-book collection by your library as

- *a one-time purchase,*
- *that is owned forever,*
- *allows for simultaneous readers,*
- *has no restrictions on printing, and*
- *can be downloaded as PDFs from within the library community.*

Our digital library collections are a great solution to beat the rising cost of textbooks. E-books can be loaded into their course management systems or onto students' e-book readers. The **Business Expert Press** digital libraries are very affordable, with no obligation to buy in future years. For more information, please visit **www.businessexpertpress.com/librarians**. To set up a trial in the United States, please email **sales@businessexpertpress.com**.